ERIC SHO

The

EQUITABLE
GUIDE TO SAVING
FOR YOUR
RETIREMENT

BLOOMSBURY

About the Author

Eric Short wrote for the *Financial Times* for over 20 years before his retirement, specialising in insurance, pensions and personal finance. He is a Fellow of the Institute of Actuaries, and now works as a freelance writer and is a lecturer in Investment at the University of Kent, Canterbury.

About The Equitable Life Assurance Society

The Equitable Life Assurance Society was founded in 1762, making it the oldest mutual life assurance society in the world, and the first to develop the sound actuarial principles on which all modern life companies are based.

Throughout its long history The Equitable has steadfastly refused to pay commission to third parties for the introduction of new business; a policy that has helped to achieve the Society's consistently low level of expenses. The Equitable today is a leader in the field of pensions for the self-employed, professionals and executives. In fact, more than half of Britain's 500 largest industrial companies have a pension arrangement with the Society.

First published 1992 by Bloomsbury Publishing Limited, 38 Soho Square, London W1V 5DF
New editions published 1994, 1996

Copyright © 1992, 1994, 1996 by Bloomsbury Publishing Plc

A CIP record for this book is available from the British Library

ISBN 0 7475 2923 X

Typeset by Hewer Text Composition Services, Edinburgh
Printed by Clays Ltd, Bungay, Suffolk

CONTENTS

ℒℰℒℰℒℰℒℰℒℰℒ

ACKNOWLEDGEMENTS

My grateful thanks go to the many people who assisted and encouraged me to write this book.

Above all, my thanks and gratitude go to my son-in-law Bruce Knox, who patiently and painstakingly guided me, a complete novice, through the intricacies of personal computers, word processors, spreadsheets and laser printers. Without his help, often given at short notice, I would have never been able to cope with the modern technology needed to write this book within its timespan.

Finally, my thanks to my wife Jean for providing constant encouragement and support, without which this book would never have been completed.

1

WHY SAVE FOR RETIREMENT?

Why save for retirement? This is a very natural question to ask when urged by life assurance salesmen, TV ads, Government officials or members of the family to make pension arrangements.

The attitude to this question, and to retirement in general, is summed up by the typical answers given to this question:

Charlie Easy-Going, a successful 44-year-old self-employed engineer, replies that the business will provide for his pension. When pressed further about savings for his old age, Charlie says that if he saves at all, then it will be for something that he can enjoy, such as a new sports car or a fantastic holiday in the West Indies, rather than for something as mundane as his future pension.

Peter Hard-Worker, a 39-year-old manager, has different reasons for not saving. He asks, in exasperation, how can he afford to save anything for his retirement with a mortgage, school fees, a large house and an estate car to keep up. He adds that he pays income tax and National Insurance contributions, which he can ill afford, so the State will provide for his retirement, and anyway with all the pressures at work and at home, he will not live long after he retires.

Susan Briteyes, Peter's secretary and personal assistant, aged 30, is honest enough to admit that she had not really thought about retirement. But anyway her husband will make provision for their old age.

David Short-Sighted, a controlling director of his family business, having just reached age 50, replies that he has started to think about retirement, but that before now the immediate problems of running the business have taken up all his time. But he adds that surely there is plenty of time to make arrangements for his pension. He is wary of dealing with life assurance companies, having heard that they overcharge on their savings plans.

These replies are typical of the general reaction of many people towards their retirement. They just do not think about it nor how they will live during retirement, until retirement is approaching.

It should be evident that the simple answer to the original question is that Charlie, Peter, Susan and David, along with most other people, will, at some time in the future, cease working full-time. When that time comes, they will find that retirement offers them a variety of activities and opportunities that are not usually available when working full-time.

To bring home this point we asked our characters to think about how they would spend their retirement.

Charlie Easy-Going's Attitude

Charlie considered that retirement would enable him to indulge in his passion for driving fast cars, following car racing in the summer and going on cruises in the winter. Asked whether such activities were expensive, Charlie agreed that they were and that he would need a good income in retirement.

Now we could ask Charlie where that income would come from. Being self-employed, he is only eligible for the basic State pension, which is currently £61.15 a week (£3,179.80 a year) for himself, and £36.60 a week (£1,903.20 a year) for his wife – a combined income of £5,083 a year. This looks pitifully small beside the £100,000 a year that Charlie is earning.

Charlie gulped at the meagre figure as he did not realise that the Government was not generous in providing pensions. But he reiterated his belief that his business would provide for his old age. He feels that when he wants to retire, he can sell his business and the proceeds will keep him in retirement. And if times are good, then Charlie should get a good price for his business. But will it be sufficient to provide an adequate income? And if there is a recession, as in recent years, will he even be able to sell the business, and at what price?

Charlie retorts that the business is his main asset and the only means of providing for his retirement. So now he is ready at least to listen to ways in which the business can provide for his retirement by saving in advance, with a big helping hand from the government in the form of generous tax reliefs.

Peter Hard-Worker's Attitude

Peter, in answer to the question of how he would spend his retirement, sighed with the thought of being able to relax and take it easy – no mortgage payments, no school-fee bills. He would have the time to go to the opera and theatre and eat out more often with his wife, and develop his hobby of collecting books.

We pointed out that Peter still had to keep up his house and garden and run the car – activities which he may have to pay other people to help with. His other intended activities would then become expensive to indulge in.

We asked Peter what he thought was an adequate income in retirement. Since he had no idea, we did some housekeeping arithmetic for him. Peter is currently earning £40,000 a year. His current net take-home earnings are approximately as follows:

Table 1. Income needs

	£
Gross earnings	40,000
less deductions:	
Income Tax	9,990
National Insurance contributions	2,112
total deductions	12,102
Take-home earnings	27,898
less outgoings ceasing on retirement:	
Mortgage payments	2,800
Travel to work	1,400
Lunches	1,100
total outgoings	5,300
Net income to maintain standards	22,598
Gross income to maintain standards	27,975

This is 70 per cent of Peter's current gross earnings. It illustrates that the usually quoted target of a pension of two-thirds of an individual's earnings is about right.

Peter accepts this figure for his income needs in retirement. But, like Charlie, he still thinks that since he has paid income tax and National Insurance contributions, then the Government will provide his pension, though he has no idea what it will be.

When Peter retires he will qualify for both the basic State pension and the full State Earnings-Related Pension Scheme (SERPS). On the present system this will amount to about £9,000 a year for himself and his wife – about one-third of what is estimated would be an adequate income.

Peter argues that he still has plenty of time to save to provide for sufficient income to keep him in comfort for the short time he will live in retirement. We have to convince him that his time before retirement is shorter than he imagines and his time in retirement far longer.

People are retiring earlier these days. But Peter still holds on to the idea that men retire at 65 and receive their pension from that age, while women retire at age 60 – the retirement ages incorporated in the State pension scheme. After all, his father recently retired at age 65. However, over the past decade or so, more and more people, particularly men, have been retiring before reaching these ages and fewer are working beyond the State retirement age. This trend is expected to continue.

This is not just hearsay or the experience of a few companies. The recession has bitten deep, as seen from the latest figures from the Department of Employment.

Table 2

| Proportion of the population in work – Men | | | | | |
Ages	1973 %	1983 %	1988 %	1993* %	2003* %
55–59	93	84	80	76	78
60–64	82	59	55	51	46
65–69	28	13	12	14	13

| Proportion of the population in work – Women | | | | | |
Ages	1973 %	1983 %	1988 %	1993* %	2003* %
55–59	51	50	53	55	56
60–64	29	20	20	23	25

* estimated
Source: Employment Gazette

Peter, looking at these figures, saw that only three out of four men aged 55 to 59 are now working, compared with nine out of ten 20 years ago, and that this proportion is expected to remain steady for the next decade. So a significant number of men have ceased work before age 60. He then noted that the decline is more dramatic in the age group 60 to 64. Twenty years ago, over four men in five were still working, but that proportion has fallen steadily during the 1980s and 1990s to its present level of one in two men.

Of even more concern to Peter was that the Department of Employment did not expect the proportion of men working between ages 60 and 64 to increase again over the next decade. He was now convinced that men were retiring early and that he should not automatically assume that he will work until age 65. He has less time to save than he thought.

Retirement can last a long time, but Peter, like most people, still thinks that retirement will be comparatively short in duration, despite the overwhelming official evidence that people, on average, are living longer.

Peter repeated the oft-quoted fact that the average lifetime of a man is 74 years, and so at 65 individuals have, on average, just nine years of their life left. But age 74 for men and 80 for women is the life expectation at birth; and this means that men and women who have survived to retirement age have a life expectation far beyond 70.

Actuaries closely monitor mortality rates as part of their professional responsibilities. They have developed specialist skills in predicting the average number of years people, having reached a certain age, can be expected to live – their life expectancies.

Table 3

Age at	Life expectancy (years)	
retirement	Men	Women
55	21.8	26.9
60	18.0	22.5
65	14.6	18.4
70	11.6	14.6

Through his work Peter knows that averages do not convey a complete picture, in this case of how long people will live in retirement. So we showed him a table, known as a life contingency table, which takes a certain number of lives for men and for women, and shows how many of those people are expected to still be alive at subsequent ages.

Table 4

Age	Number of people living to age	
	Men	Women
60	100,000	100,000
65	90,678	95,705
70	77,867	88,754
75	61,475	77,993
80	42,671	62,550
85	24,372	43,019
90	10,409	22,950
95	2,912	8,132
100	448	1,529

Source: Actuarial table PA(90)

Thus if Peter retires at 60 he has a three-in-four chance of reaching age 70, a two-in-five chance of reaching age 80 and nearly a one-in-ten chance of reaching age 90. If he retires at age 65, he has a 17 out of 20 chance of reaching age 70, almost evens of reaching age 80 and a one-in-ten chance of reaching age 90. He has almost the same chance of living to age 90 as of dying before age 70.

For women, the odds are much higher. A woman retiring at age 60 has nearly a nine-in-ten chance of reaching age 70, nearly a two-in-three chance of reaching age 80 and nearly a one-in-four chance of reaching age 90.

The overall effect of providing a high level of retirement income over a long period means that pensions are not cheap to buy.

To secure for Peter at 65 the gross annual income of 27,975 increasing by 5 per cent a year, with half the income to his wife on his death, would currently cost around £440,000 to buy an annuity from a leading life company. Peter argues that he has given and will continue to give good service to his employer, and surely the company will help him out in his retirement by providing the pension.

Many employers *do* run good occupational pension schemes, but they are not obliged to do so. Certainly, the company is not obliged under any circumstances to give Peter, or more likely his widow, financial help after he has retired. Companies are taking an increasingly hard line over employees who could have joined the company pension scheme but chose not to do so.

David Short-Sighted's Attitude

David's life has to date been completely tied up in his family business. This has involved him in travelling to various parts of the world. This has whetted his interest to revisit those countries as a tourist to see the countries and their places of interest at leisure, not in haste as a businessman.

Hence he has started to dream about his retirement and appreciates that he will need an adequate income to realise those dreams. But like Charlie Easy-Going, David feels that the family business will provide him with that income in retirement.

David considers that all he needs to do is to remain as a controlling director and continue to draw director's fees, while leaving his son to run the business. But being a sleeping partner in the business could impose a severe strain on its cash flow in times like the present, and it could cause all kinds of problems for his son.

There are far better ways of using the resources of the business to provide for David's income in retirement, without relying on chance or imposing financial burdens on the next generation. Above all, there are generous tax concessions available if David saves for his pension, reducing the company's tax bill.

Susan Briteyes' Attitude

Susan, being young, has simply never considered retirement, and her attitude up to now has been to leave all financial matters to her husband.

If Susan's husband is in a good occupational pension scheme, or has taken out adequate life cover, Susan will be provided for financially should she suffer the misfortune to be widowed before retirement. But if both Susan and her husband survive to retirement, and he is in a good occupational pension scheme, then under the present circumstances their financial situation in retirement will change from a two-person income to a one-and-a-bit-person income, since Susan will only receive the State pension. If her husband has not made any pension arrangements, their income would drop dramatically in retirement.

Although Susan accepts that there is a need to save towards her retirement, she feels that there is plenty of time later to make any arrangements.

After apathy, delay is the major obstacle to overcome in persuading individuals, like our four characters, to save for their retirement. It is so easy for everybody to make excuses that they cannot afford to save just at this moment, and to delude themselves into thinking that there is plenty of time and that they will start to save when they have cash to spare.

Delay means quite simply that the later one starts, the less time there is for the fund to accumulate, and a lower fund means a lower pension.

The following table indicates the effects of delay. It assumes that an individual saves £1,000 a year towards a pension at age 65 and that the investment grows at 12 per cent a year, less the various management charges levied by the company.

Table 5

Age Starting to Save	Accumulated Fund £
30	409,000
35	234,000
40	132,000
45	73,300
50	39,000

Source: Equitable Life

It should now be clear to everybody that:

- People, in general, are retiring at an earlier age than their fathers.
- Retirement can last a long time.
- Retirement offers people the opportunity to do a variety of activities not available when working.

These points should emphasise that people will need an income in retirement comparable with the income they received while at work.

It is necessary to expel the belief that someone else would automatically provide a retirement income, whether it is the Government, the family business or the employer.

For many people, and particularly the higher earners, they will have to save for that retirement income while they are working.

And they will find that the Government gives considerable help through generous tax incentives. Such savings must be started as early as possible before retirement; delay can result in an inadequate income.

2

ℒℰℒℰℒℰℒℰℒℰℒℰ

THE PENSIONS FRAMEWORK

Before anyone starts on a journey, they need to consult the map, plan their route and check on the services available if they want a trouble-free journey and to arrive safely. Similarly, in planning to save for retirement, an individual will need to understand the existing pensions framework in the UK, what it offers and, above all, what it does not offer.

Like many maps, the pensions situation in this country is extremely complex and difficult for the uninitiated to understand, the difficulties compounded by a plethora of legislation. One way of looking at it is by considering the overall pension as being made up of a series of tiers or layers that build up to the retirement income. The main features of each tier should apply to the majority of people, and are comparable with the main roads on a map. But many people will also be affected by secondary features of the components of the pensions framework, comparable with having to travel on a map's sideroads.

The First Tier

The first tier is the basic State pension, and this is the foundation of an individual's income in retirement. All people in work who pay National Insurance contributions are eligible for this basic pension. Payment of National Insurance contributions is compulsory, and as there is no tax relief on them for employees or the self-employed, effectively these contributions are taxes on top of income tax.

The main features of the basic State pension are:

- **The pension is paid weekly at the same amount to everyone who has paid sufficient contributions. It forms part of an individual's taxable income.**

- The current basic level is £61.15 a week for a single person, paid from age 65 for men and 60 for women, the normal State pension age (see page 12).
- A married woman with a nil or inadequate contribution record is entitled to a pension on her husband's contribution record, but paid from the time when her husband takes his basic pension, providing she has reached or passed age 60. The current payment is £36.60 a week. If she is under 60, she has to wait until that age before claiming her pension, but if she is not working, or earning less than £48.25 a week, then her husband receives the pension until she is 60.
- Individuals have the right to defer taking the basic State pension for up to five years, qualifying for a higher pension the longer the pension is deferred. The pension must be taken when men reach age 70 and when women reach 65.
- However, the pension cannot be taken before a man reaches age 65 or a woman reaches age 60 even though they may have finished work before reaching State pension age. This can have serious implications for employees forced to take early retirement, since they have to wait until reaching the State pension age before receiving any pension from the State.
- The pension is currently increased each April in line with the 12-monthly rise in the Retail Price Index at the previous September. Thus the real value of the pension is maintained against inflation.

Jack Careful retiring at 65 receives a basic State pension of £61.15 a week. His wife Jill, aged 62 and with no National Insurance contribution record, will receive immediately a pension of £36.60 a week – a combined basic State pension of £97.75 a week for the family, which can be paid on one pension book.

His twin brother, Colin Careful, also retiring at 65, receives the £61.15 a week basic pension. His wife Cora has only a little contribution record, but since she is aged 58 and working, she has to wait until she reaches age 60 before receiving the pension. However, if she was not working, then Colin would receive a further £36.60 weekly pension until Cora became eligible for the pension at age 60.

Their elder brother, Brian Careful, has deferred taking his pension until age 70. He receives £83.95 a week, with his wife Barbara, aged 65, having no contribution record, receiving £63.53 a week.

State Pension Age

As stated, the State pension age, that is the age at which people are entitled to receive retirement pensions from the State, is currently 65 for men and 60 for women. However, the Government has enacted legislation which will bring about a common State pension age for men and women at age 65. But the change will not start until May 2010 and will be phased in over the period to April 2020. So women born before 6th April 1950 will still be able to receive their State pension from age 60, while all women born on or after 6th March 1995 will receive their State pension from age 65. Women born between these dates will have a State pension age between 60 and 65. Table 6 shows the phasing-in timetable and which women are affected.

For example, a woman born on 20th September 1952 would have a State pension age of 62 years and 6 months and would qualify for a State pension from 20th March 2015.

The facility for deferring receiving the State pension for up to five years would still apply.

The Second Tier

At this stage the Inland Revenue enters the pensions framework.

The Self-employed

Self-employed people are only obliged to belong to the first-tier basic State pension. The second tier in their pension arrangements is personal pensions and it is entirely voluntary whether a self-employed person saves through a personal pension and, if so, how much they save.

As seen already, the basic State pension is extremely low. If, in the above example, Jack Careful was self-employed with earnings of £40,000 a year, the combined basic State pension to himself and his wife of £5,083 a year (£97.75 a week) is less than 13 per cent of his

Table 6. Phase-In of State Pension Age for Women

Date of Birth	State Pension Age Year Month
up to 5th April 1950	60 years
6th April 1950 – 5th May 1950	60 years 1 month
6th May 1950 – 5th June 1950	60 years 2 months
6th June 1950 – 5th July 1950	60 years 3 months
6th July 1950 – 5th August 1950	60 years 4 months
6th August 1950 – 5th September 1950	60 years 5 months
6th September 1950 – 5th October 1950	60 years 6 months
6th October 1950 – 5th November 1950	60 years 7 months
6th November 1950 – 5th December 1950	60 years 8 months
6th December 1950 – 5th January 1951	60 years 9 months
6th January 1951 – 5th February 1951	60 years 10 months
6th February 1951 – 5th March 1951	60 years 11 months
6th March 1951 – 5th April 1951	61 years
6th April 1951 – 5th May 1951	61 years 1 month
6th May 1951 – 5th June 1951	61 years 2 months
6th June 1951 – 5th July 1951	61 years 3 months
6th July 1951 – 5th August 1951	61 years 4 months
6th August 1951 – 5th September 1951	61 years 5 months
6th September 1951 – 5th October 1951	61 years 6 months
6th October 1951 – 5th November 1951	61 years 7 months
6th November 1951 – 5th December 1951	61 years 8 months
6th December 1951 – 5th January 1952	61 years 9 months
6th January 1952 – 5th February 1952	61 years 10 months
6th February 1952 – 5th March 1952	61 years 11 months
6th March 1952 – 5th April 1952	62 years
6th April 1952 – 5th May 1952	62 years 1 month
6th May 1952 – 5th June 1952	62 years 2 months
6th June 1952 – 5th July 1952	62 years 3 months
6th July 1952 – 5th August 1952	62 years 4 months
6th August 1952 – 5th September 1952	62 years 5 months
6th September 1952 – 5th October 1952	62 years 6 months
6th October 1952 – 5th November 1952	62 years 7 months
6th November 1952 – 5th December 1952	62 years 8 months
6th December 1952 – 5th January 1953	62 years 9 months
6th January 1953 – 5th February 1953	62 years 10 months
6th February 1953 – 5th March 1953	62 years 11 months
6th March 1953 – 5th April 1953	63 years
6th April 1953 – 5th May 1953	63 years 1 month
6th May 1953 – 5th June 1953	63 years 2 months
6th June 1953 – 5th July 1953	63 years 3 months
6th July 1953 – 5th August 1953	63 years 4 months
6th August 1953 – 5th September 1953	63 years 5 months
6th September 1953 – 5th October 1953	63 years 6 months
6th October 1953 – 5th November 1953	63 years 7 months
6th November 1953 – 5th December 1953	63 years 8 months
6th December 1953 – 5th January 1954	63 years 9 months
6th January 1954 – 5th February 1954	63 years 10 months
6th February 1954 – 5th March 1954	63 years 11 months
6th March 1954 – 5th April 1954	64 years
6th April 1954 – 5th May 1954	64 years 1 month
6th May 1954 – 5th June 1954	64 years 2 months
6th June 1954 – 5th July 1954	64 years 3 months
6th July 1954 – 5th August 1954	64 years 4 months
6th August 1954 – 5th September 1954	64 years 5 months

Date of Birth	State Pension Age Year Month
6th September 1954 – 5th October 1954	64 years 6 months
6th October 1954 – 5th November 1954	64 years 7 months
6th November 1954 – 5th December 1954	64 years 8 months
6th December 1954 – 5th January 1955	64 years 9 months
6th January 1955 – 5th February 1955	64 years 10 months
6th February 1955 – 5th March 1955	64 years 11 months
6th March 1955 and later	65 years

earnings: he should have already made substantial savings through personal pensions.

Personal pensions for the self-employed will be described in detail in the next section, including the tax incentives provided by the Inland Revenue to help one save for retirement.

The Employed

A second-tier pension is compulsory for those in employment, although most employees have a choice of pension arrangement within the existing pensions framework, in addition to the compulsory National Insurance contributions.

The central pillar of the second tier is the State Earnings-Related Pension Scheme, always referred to as SERPS, except by civil servants who use the official name of Additional Pensions. The scheme is dealt with in more detail in the next section. The employee and the employer each pay National Insurance contributions, with no tax relief on the employee's contributions, at the basic contribution rate of 10 per cent for employees and 10.2 per cent for employers for the basic pension and SERPS. The actual contribution scale is complex, depending on the employee's earnings.

There are three alternatives to SERPS:

- Employers can take their employees out of SERPS, known as 'contracting-out', with an occupational pension scheme set up by the company for their employees.
- Employees not in a company scheme can contract-out of SERPS through an Appropriate Personal Pension.
- Employees in a company scheme which is not contracted-out can contract-out themselves with an Appropriate Personal Pension.

The various schemes used to contract-out of SERPS must provide benefits that are equivalent to or better than those provided by SERPS. If the employee, or the employer, does nothing, then by default he or she is automatically in SERPS.

Employees and their employers who contract-out of SERPS get a reduction in their National Insurance contributions, known as a rebate. And the contributions paid by the employee into an alternative pension arrangement get tax relief from the Inland Revenue.

The Third Tier

The third-tier pension arrangements are on a voluntary basis by the employee or his employer, and these arrangements depend very much on the second-tier decisions. Again, tax relief is given on the contributions to these voluntary schemes.

The diagram below sets out the third-tier structure, which can be summarised as follows:

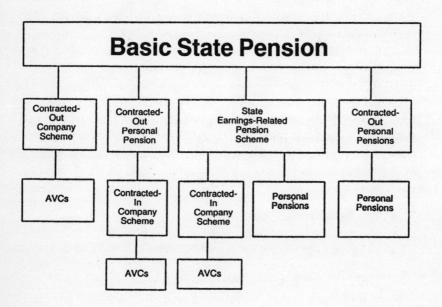

Second Tier – SERPS

- The employer can have an occupational pension scheme on top of SERPS.
- The employee not in a company occupational scheme can have a personal pension on top of SERPS.

Second Tier – Occupational Scheme

The employee can boost his pension by paying extra contributions into an AVC (Additional Voluntary Contribution) scheme.

Technically, an employee in an occupational pension scheme cannot take out a personal pension. However, in many respects an AVC scheme can be regarded as an employee's personal pension.

Second Tier – Appropriate Personal Pension Contracted-out of SERPS

The employee can take out a personal pension arrangement.

An employee who has contracted-out of SERPS with a special personal pension will be in his employer's occupational scheme for the third tier. He can take out an AVC arrangement as a fourth tier.

So how does this framework apply to Peter Hard-Worker, Susan Briteyes and David Short-Sighted, employees who have at last decided to save for their retirement?

Peter is a line manager, and if his firm has an occupational pension scheme contracted-out of SERPS which he joins, then he has:

- first tier – basic State pension
- second tier – company occupational pension
- third tier – pension secured by AVCs.

If, however, Peter decides to make his own pension arrangements, or his firm does not have a pension scheme, then:

either he saves by
- first tier – basic State pension,
- second tier – SERPS,
- third tier – personal pension,

or he saves by
- first tier – basic State pension,
- second tier – appropriate personal pension,
- third tier – personal pension.

A similar structure applies to Susan, Peter's secretary.

David Short-Sighted is a controlling director in the family business. He could do the same as Peter, but an alternative is available to him:

- first tier – basic State pension,
- second tier – SERPS,
- third tier – an executive company pension arrangement.

This description of the UK pensions framework assumes that the employee remains in one job with one employer throughout his or her working life, and that a self-employed person remains self-employed.

But life is never as simple as that. People change jobs, some employers have occupational schemes while others do not, employees become self-employed and vice versa, and employees can contract-out of SERPS and go back into SERPS.

3

*H*ow *pension arrangements work*

Our intrepid heroes and heroine are now looking into saving for retirement. Now that they are aware of the current framework for pension provision in the UK they are interested in knowing more about how the various elements in that framework operate.

This is the right attitude to take and it is important to get a feel for the various pension arrangements available. It is too easy to rush out and take the first pension plan offered by an enthusiastic salesman or join a company scheme without any further thought, which could result in a savings arrangement that is both inefficient and one with which one is unhappy. And it is difficult and expensive to unravel an existing plan.

We all need a broad understanding of how schemes work, in order to put together the most suitable plan to meet our own requirements; pension schemes and pension contracts are more complex than simply paying contributions and drawing the pension. When a pension arrangement is being considered the salient features to look for are:

- Whether the level of pension is pre-determined.
- What provision is made for increases in the pension once it becomes payable.
- What protection is provided for spouses and children when the individual dies.
- The investment requirements.
- What the phases in the operation of the pension arrangement entail, including:
- Paying the contributions – how much should be paid and how often?
- Investing the contributions and accumulated fund – where should the assets be invested?
- What benefits are secured at retirement or earlier?

With the State scheme and with occupational schemes it is the Government and the employer respectively who have to take the decisions on the various phases – how much to pay, what benefits to provide and where to invest the assets. The employee has no involvement or responsibility or influence in the State scheme, and usually very little in his occupational scheme.

But with any type of personal pension, the individual has to take the decisions. And the amount of pension at the end of the day will depend on the decisions taken and how successfully they were carried out. So an understanding of how pension schemes work is essential in order to secure an adequate income in retirement.

There are two basic formats for pension arrangements: defined benefits and defined contributions.

Defined Benefits

As implied by the name, with this type of arrangement the pension benefits are defined, either fixed as with the basic State pension, current value of £61.15 a week for a single person; or in terms of an employee's earnings, as with SERPS or with the majority of occupational pension schemes. As such, the benefits can be calculated, approximately, in advance of retirement, in money terms or as a proportion of an employee's earnings.

Having defined the benefits, the amount of contribution payments needed to provide these benefits is determined, usually by an actuary. Defined benefit schemes can only be realistically operated on a collective basis, such as with a State scheme or an employer's occupational scheme.

Defined Contributions

Such schemes are usually known as 'money purchase' schemes in the UK. Under this arrangement, the amount of the contributions paid is determined in advance, either deliberately or by chance. These contributions are invested and a fund built up. At the time of retirement, this fund is used either to buy a pension from a life company or to provide income with an annuity bought later.

The individual has no idea until the time of retirement of the amount of his pension, either in money terms or as a proportion of his earnings. The amount of pension will depend on:

- the number and amount of contributions paid,
- the investment performance during the time preceding when the benefits are taken,
- annuity rates at the time the benefits are taken.

Personal pensions, most AVC schemes and some company occupational schemes, including executive pension arrangements, operate on a defined contribution or money purchase basis.

We can now look at the various pension arrangements which make up the UK pensions framework.

The first-tier basic State pension was discussed in chapter two, so we start with the centrepiece of the second tier – SERPS. This section is relevant to Peter Hard-Worker, Susan Briteyes and David Short-Sighted, simply because they are in SERPS. However, Charlie Easy-Going, being self-employed, is not really interested in SERPS.

State Earnings-Related Pension Scheme

This scheme is invariably referred to as SERPS, although Additional Pension is used in the official DSS literature.

If the basic State pension scheme seemed complicated in its operation and entitlement, then SERPS is virtually incomprehensible, and surveys indicate that many employees still do not appreciate that they are in the scheme, let alone understand it. This is certainly the case with Peter, Susan and David.

The situation is made even more complex because two variations of the scheme are currently in operation.

SERPS was introduced in 1978 by the Labour Government, and was designed to provide a pension of 25 per cent of an employee's earnings averaged over the best 20 years. Thus a full pension would be earned after the employee had paid only 20 years' contributions; that is, those employees reaching State pension age on or after April 1998 would qualify for a full pension.

But the scheme was radically revised in 1988 by the Conservative Government, with benefits being severely cut back. Full pension entitlement will now be only 20 per cent of earnings averaged over an employee's working life – men with 49 years' contributions and women with 44 years. So only employees starting work at age 16 and paying National Insurance contributions can qualify for a full

SERPS pension under the revised system. However, there is a new benefit structure, being phased in over 49 years from 1988, which means that:

- Employees reaching State pension age on or before the financial year 1998/1999 will have their pension based on the old system.
- Men reaching State pension age of 65 on or after the year 2037/2038 and women reaching State pension age of 60 on or after the year 2032/2033 will be in the new system.
- The benefit structure will be phased in for those employees reaching State pension age in the intervening years, based on the actual number of years' contributions made from 1978 up to State pension age.

The main features of the present benefits structure include:

- The pension is paid at the State pension age of 65 for men and 60 for women, with the option to defer payment for up to five years on the same terms as for the basic State pension.
- It is a defined benefit arrangement, with the pension entitlement being based on 20 per cent of an employee's weekly earnings averaged over his or her working life since April 1978, or if later, since the beginning of the financial year in which he or she is 16. Only earnings in a complete financial year count towards the SERPS pension.

The entitlement is not based on an employee's total earnings, but only on the earnings in the band between a lower and an upper limit. The current Lower Earnings Limit is £61 a week (£3,172 a year) and the Upper Earnings Limit is £455 a week (£23,660 a year). These limits are increased each year in line with inflation.

Therefore an employee earning £60 a week in 1996/1997 would not have any SERPS entitlement for the year; an employee earning £100 a week would have his SERPS pension for the year based on £39 while an employee earning £250 a week would have his SERPS pension based on £189. Someone earning £455 or more a week would have his or her SERPS pension for the year based on £394, no matter how high their earnings were.

- The employee's earnings in the band for each successive year are revalued annually in line with the rise in National Average Earnings up to State pension age.

- Each revalued year's earnings are added together and the total divided by a factor, representing the employee's working life, to get the average earnings.

Under the original Labour scheme, the earnings would have been averaged over an employee's best 20 years and the SERPS pension was 25 per cent of this average. Under the present scheme, earnings are averaged over the whole working life and the SERPS pension is 20 per cent of this average.

In the phase-in period, employees get 25 per cent of their average earnings between 1978 and 1988 and a phased-in fraction for average earnings after that date.

- Widows qualify for their husband's full SERPS pension if their husband dies before 2000, but only 50 per cent if he dies after then. Widowers only inherit their wife's pension if they are over State pension age when she dies.
- The pension, when payable, is revalued each year in line with the rise in the Retail Price Index, thereby keeping its value against inflation.

Hopefully the following examples will clarify the situation. They all relate to men currently earning £40,000 a year. As such, their weekly earnings are well above the Upper Earnings Limit and so their earnings each year for the SERPS pension will be based on the full banded earnings for that year. The SERPS pension is quoted in current money values, assuming that the employee's earnings since 1978 have always been above the upper limit and that for simplicity the earnings band before and after this year has been equivalent to the present value of £394 a week:

Employee A retires in 1998/1999

His SERPS pension is calculated on the old benefit structure. He has completed the 20-year period for a full pension and it will be based on the full banded earnings. In each of the 20 years, he has had band earnings equivalent to £394 a week in current money values, so his average earnings are £394 a week (£20,488 a year). His SERPS pension will be 25 per cent of this average, that is £98.50 a week (£5,122 a year). Thus the combined basic and SERPS pension, including the wife's basic pension, is £5,083 + £5,122 = £10,205; that is, just over one-quarter of employee A's earnings of £40,000.

Employee B retires in 2037/2038

He has just started work for the family business at the age of 19. He will complete 46 years of contributions to SERPS, paying band earnings of £394 a week in current money values. His SERPS pension will be calculated completely on the new rules. So his average weekly earnings will be: 46/49ths of £394 = £369.88. The SERPS pension will be 20 per cent of this average, that is £73.97 a week (£3,846 a year), a reduction of a quarter compared with the SERPS pension for employee A. The combined basic and SERPS pension for employee B will be £5,083 + £3,846 = £8,929 a year, just over one-fifth of his earnings.

Peter Hard-Worker

For our third example, we return to Peter, who since he has as yet made no pension arrangements, will be relying on the State for his pension. Peter is nearing his 40th birthday, and so will reach age 65 in 2016/2017 – the intermediate years. He will have paid 10 years of contributions to 1988 and will pay a further 28 full years' contributions until age 65 – a total of 38 full years' contributions since April 1978, with all payments falling within the full band earnings of £394 a week in current values. The SERPS pension calculation is in two parts:

(a) Contributions from 1978 to 1988 – 10 years' paid
     Average earnings = 10/38 of 394 = £103.68
     SERPS pension = 25% of 103.68 = £25.92.
(b) Contributions from 1988 to 2016 – 28 years' paid
     Average earnings = 28/38 of 394 = £290.31
     SERPS pension = 20% of 290.31 = £58.06.

Total SERPS pension = a + b = £83.98 a week (£4,367 a year). So Peter Hard-Worker, relying on the State, can expect a pension of £5,083 + £4,367 = £9,450 a year for himself and his wife (assuming she has no pension in her own right) – less than one-quarter of his earnings.

Readers, particularly the higher-paid, should by now be convinced that the State does not provide an adequate pension.

The above examples are comparatively straightforward; many employees, like Susan Briteyes, have earnings below the Upper

Limit, that vary from week to week and during the financial year. It would be a difficult task for people in a similar position to Susan to even guess at their SERPS pension entitlement, although they can obtain a quotation of their SERPS benefit to date, and an estimate of their total SERPS pension, from the Department of Social Security, by filling in form BR19 (obtainable from the local DSS office) and sending it to the address on the form.

All employees currently in SERPS should obtain a quotation as the starting point of planning their retirement income.

Now it is time to consider the structure of the various second-tier alternatives to SERPS.

Occupational Pension Schemes

This is the generic title for pension arrangements set up by employers for the benefit of some or all of their employees, including the public sector pension schemes established by the Government, public bodies and local authorities for their employees.

Until 1988, employers could force employees into the pension scheme by making membership a condition of employment. Now employees have the final decision as to whether or not they belong to their employer's pension scheme.

All public sector schemes and the majority of occupational schemes provided by large and medium-sized companies operate on a defined benefits basis, with the pension being related to an employee's earnings at or near retirement, and as such are invariably referred to as final salary schemes. Most are contracted-out of SERPS.

However, a sizeable number of company schemes operate on the defined contribution or money purchase principle.

Occupational pension schemes provide a whole range of benefits, not only to employees, but to their spouses and dependents, usually children up to the age of 18 or still in full-time higher education. These are:

Benefits

- Pension to the employee on retirement, whether retirement is at the normal age, early, late or through ill health.

- Pension to the spouse on the death of the employee after retirement.
- Benefits on the death of the employee before retirement consisting of a tax-free cash sum, plus a pension to the spouse and payments to dependants, usually children of the employee.
- A deferred pension to employees leaving the service of the employer.

Contributions

The employee's contributions are pre-determined, usually as a percentage of earnings, and are independent of the benefits. The employer pays the balance of the cost of operating the scheme and paying the benefits. The employee gets tax relief at his or her top rate on the contributions, thereby reducing the overall cost to the employee.

In many schemes, employees pay no contributions. Such schemes are known as non-contributory schemes, with the employer paying for the entire cost of the scheme.

Trust Deeds and Rules

Company pension schemes come in all shapes and sizes, with very few schemes being identical. Variations occur in the pension age, the definition of earnings on which the benefits are calculated, treatment of early and late retirement, and the actual benefits provided by the scheme.

Company schemes are invariably set up under trust and the operation of the scheme will be governed by the trust deed and rules. The deed and rules will set out the benefits and define the terms on which those benefits are calculated.

Limits and Restrictions

The trust deed and rules must take into account the various restrictions and limits imposed on schemes by the authorities – the Inland Revenue and the Department of Social Security. If the scheme is being used to contract-out of SERPS, then it must provide a minimum level of benefit, at least equivalent to the amount by which the SERPS benefit is reduced as a result of contracting-out. The restrictions and limits imposed by the Inland Revenue on all occupational schemes are of the most significance to the operation of schemes and to their members. The most important restrictions are:

- The ceiling on an employee's earnings, known as the 'Cap', that can be used for pension benefits and qualify for tax relief. The current ceiling is £82,200 and it is usually revalued each year in line with the annual rise in the Retail Price Index, although it was not increased for 1993/94. It applies to all employees in schemes set up from 14 March 1989 and all employees joining existing schemes from 1 June 1989.
- Accrual period, the minimum permissible period for an employee to acquire maximum pension and maximum cash sum at retirement, is 20 years.
- The maximum permissible pension before taking any cash is two-thirds of final earnings subject to the Cap.
- The maximum cash sum at retirement is one-and-a-half times final earnings, subject to the Cap as above.
- The maximum death-in-service cash sum is four times the earnings at the time of death, subject to the Cap as above.
- The maximum spouses' pension is two-thirds the employee's pension.
- The maximum contribution which an employee can make to an occupational scheme is 15 per cent of earnings, subject to the Cap as above.

Many of the Inland Revenue restrictions affect highly-paid employees, particularly someone like David Short-Sighted.

However, Peter and Susan, as well as David, are affected by the restrictions which set the maximum level of benefit for both pension and cash sum payments, and the rate at which those benefits can be built up. The main features of a typical company occupational pension scheme (a final salary scheme), can be summarised as:

- Who can join the scheme.
- At what age the pension becomes payable.
- The basis for calculating the various pension benefits.
- Benefits on death of employee before retirement.
- Investments of the scheme.
- Trustees' discretionary powers.

Membership

It is rare for employees to be able to join a company pension scheme the moment they start work for an employer. There is usually a minimum age, it can be as low as 20 or as high as 30, and/ or a minimum period, six months or more, and an employee usually has to work a minimum number of hours a week before he or she is eligible for membership of the scheme. The conditions must be the same for men and women, and are designed to ensure that the scheme is not cluttered with members who only stayed a short time with the company, and excludes the part-time employees who only work a few hours a week. In addition, the scheme usually excludes those employees who are within a given period, usually five years, of the pension age.

As stated, employers cannot make membership of the scheme a condition of employment for eligible employees, but they can make membership voluntary, so that the employee has to apply to join. Alternatively employers can make membership of the scheme automatic for eligible employees and the employee has to apply to opt out of the scheme. Since apathy is an important factor in many people's attitude towards pensions, if employees have to apply to join, then they do nothing, and similarly, if employees have to apply to leave the scheme, they generally stay in the scheme.

Pension Age

Company pension schemes have, or are in the process of introducing, a common normal pension age. However, such pension ages vary between schemes. The latest survey of schemes by the National Association of Pension Funds shows that nearly 60 per cent of schemes have a pension age of 65 and nearly 30 per cent have a pension age of 60. Most of the remaining schemes have a pension age of either 62 or 63. Only a very small number have pension ages of 61 or 64.

Earnings

Practice varies considerably regarding an employee's earnings on which his or her pension is based, known as pensionable earnings. It can be an employee's full earnings, or earnings less an allowance for the basic State pension (one or one-and-a-half times the basic pension). It can just include an employee's basic earnings or it can include overtime, bonus payments, commission, and so on. The earnings may relate to those at the time of the employee's retirement, or at a date some time during the year prior to retirement or even the average of the best three years out of the last ten years, each year's earnings being revalued in line with the Retail Price Index. The Inland Revenue permits a very wide definition of earnings.

Accrual of the Pension

Although employees can acquire the maximum pension after 20 years' service, the majority of occupational schemes require employees to complete 40 years' membership to build to the maximum pension.

The common structure found in the majority of company occupational schemes is for an employee to build up his pension year by year, like a series of building bricks, with each year's membership providing the employee with a specific pension entitlement expressed as a fraction of final salary. A frequent build-up is for the employee to be entitled to 1/60th of final salary for each year of membership of the scheme or service with the company. Thus, an employee with 40 years' service with his employer would have built up a pension entitlement of 40/60ths, that is two-thirds of the final salary – the maximum permissible.

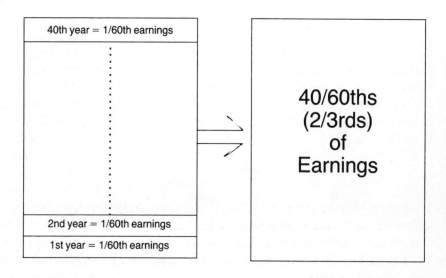

But comparatively few employees stay 40 years with one employer. For example, the employer of Peter Hard-Worker and Susan Briteyes, Forward Enterprises, has a scheme with pension ages of 65 for men and women. Peter, aged 39, could complete 25 full years' membership by age 65 and would be entitled to a pension of 25/60ths of final salary – less than half – from the company pension scheme. Susan, aged 30, could complete 35 full years' membership by age 65 and would be entitled to a pension of 35/60ths of final salary from the company scheme. It is obviously advantageous to start saving for retirement early.

Some employers are less generous in the pension build-up, offering 1/80th of final salary for each year of membership, with a maximum pension of 40/80ths (one half) after 40 years' service.

Cash Sum at Retirement

When employees in a company occupational scheme retire, they have the option to convert part of their pension into a tax-free cash sum, known as commuting part of the pension. The Inland Revenue have strict rules over the maximum cash sum that can be paid and the terms for converting pension into cash. Although it is only an option, and employees do not have to commute any part of their pension, to date well over 90 per cent of employees on retirement do take the maximum cash sum permitted, thereby reinforcing the belief that the cash sum is an inbuilt benefit.

In public sector occupational schemes, such as the civil service scheme, the tax-free cash sum is an inbuilt benefit. The benefit build-up for such schemes is 3/80ths cash and 1/80th pension, both relating to final salary, for each year of membership, with a maximum of 40 years' benefit, that is a cash sum of one-and-a-half times final salary and a pension of one-half of final salary. This is equivalent to a maximum two-thirds pension on a company scheme.

Pension Increases

Public service schemes provide for all pensions to be automatically increased each year in line with the rise in the Retail Price Index, thus making the pensions inflation-proof.

Pension increases provided by company schemes vary considerably between schemes:

- From April 1997, all schemes must guarantee that pensions are increased each year in line with the rise in the Retail Price Index up to a maximum of 5 per cent a year (known as Limited Price Indexation or LPI). But this will only apply to pensions accrued from April 1997. So ultimately company pensions will be inflation-proofed provided the annual rate of inflation does not exceed 5 per cent.

  It is up to the trustees of individual schemes to decide whether to increase the whole pension in line with LPI. Many schemes already do so, while others may well do so.

- Many schemes already guarantee automatic pension increases each year, irrespective of the rate of inflation, usually 3, 4 or 5 per cent.

- Trustees often have the power to give discretionary increases over and above any guarantees or legal requirements up to the increase in the Retail Price Index. The ability to do this will depend on the financial position of the scheme.

Spouse's Pension

Occupational schemes provide an automatic spouse's pension on the death of the employee after he or she has retired, though universal payment of pensions to widowers has only been introduced comparatively recently. The maximum spouse's pension is two-thirds of the employee's pension, but the usual payment is half the employee's pension. In all cases, the spouse's pension is based on the employee's full pension before any part is commuted for a cash sum. If the spouse dies first, the employee's pension is maintained in full, but if the employee dies first, the pension is reduced. This is just one of many anomalies in benefits provided by company pension schemes.

Early Retirement

If any employee retires before the stated pension age, the pension is reduced in two ways. First, there are fewer years for the pension to accrue. For example, if Peter Hard-Worker wants to retire at 60 instead of 65, he will only have accrued 20 years' service, instead of

25, and his pension would be based on 20/60ths of his pensionable earnings at 60.

Second, some schemes make a further reduction on this reduced pension, to reflect the fact that the scheme has received fewer contributions, in this case almost five years less, and will have to pay the pension for a longer period – almost five years more. This second reduction, on an actuarial basis, can be as high as 5 or 6 per cent for each year retirement is taken earlier than normal. Thus Peter retiring at 60 could suffer a further actuarial reduction of 25 to 30 per cent on an already reduced pension. Many schemes are more generous than this to employees retiring early, especially if the employee is taking redundancy through early retirement. The early reduction factors may be as low as 1 or 2 per cent a year, or in some schemes there may be a zero reduction.

Late Retirement

The usual practice is to accumulate the employee's pension accrued at normal pension age by a fixed percentage.

It is important to note that employees do not have flexibility over the payment of the pension. If they reach pension age and cease work, then they must take the pension. Neither can they take the pension before the normal pension age while still working for the employer.

Death-in-Service

This is a valuable series of benefits provided by occupational schemes to the families of employees, such as Peter, who are married with children. These benefits are:

- A cash sum based on a multiple of an employee's pensionable earnings, up to four times those earnings subject to the limits stated above.
- A spouse's pension usually, but not necessarily, based on the employee's earnings at the time of his or her death and the employee's prospective service up to the normal pension age. Thus, if Peter should die shortly after joining a company scheme, his wife would receive a widow's pension based on 25/60ths of his pensionable earnings.
- A pension paid to the children until they reach age 18 or cease full-time education after 18. The cash sum for the

spouse and the spouse's pension benefits are not applicable for a single employee, yet there is rarely an adjustment in the employee's contribution; this is another anomaly.

Early Leavers

The position of employees changing jobs is explained in chapter ten.

Indeed, final salary schemes contain a number of inequalities, with married employees doing better than single employees, higher-paid employees doing comparatively better than lower-paid, women doing better than men with comparative service, and employees who stay doing better than those who leave.

Investments

The investment of the assets is the responsibility of the trustees, who will invariably employ investment managers. The investments will cover the whole range – equities, property, fixed-interest and cash. The benefits, being related to an employee's final salary, are not directly dependent on the investment performance of the scheme's assets. The employer carries the investment risk and covers any shortfall in investment performance to meet the liabilities.

If the investment performance is so poor that the resulting shortfall is too large for the employer to cover, then the benefits could be reduced. And pensioners will be concerned that the investment performance is good, so that the scheme is in a financially healthy position for the trustees to pay discretionary pension increases.

Money Purchase Company Schemes

David Short-Sighted is now interested, since executive pension arrangements are essentially money purchase company schemes, although many main company schemes are also on a money purchase basis.

These schemes appear comparatively straightforward in operation compared with final salary schemes.

The phases of operation in a money purchase scheme are:

- The contributions are paid in respect of each employee.
- These contributions are invested.
- The accumulated fund for each employee is, at the time of his or her retirement, used to provide a pension by buying an annuity from a life company.

Each employee has his or her own individual account. So when an employee leaves a job, he or she can take the accumulated value of the account with them, making money purchase schemes fully transferable when employees change jobs.

Contributions

The usual form of contributions is either a fixed contribution as a percentage of earnings from both employees and employers, or banded contributions as a percentage of earnings, with the percentage increasing with each age band. The same contribution rate applies to men and women.

Investments

Investments are usually done on a collective basis. The vast majority of employers arrange their company money purchase schemes through life companies, with the company being responsible for the investments and administration. In some schemes there is scope for employees to have some choice in the underlying investments.

The amount of pension secured for an employee at retirement depends on the size of the accumulated fund and annuity rates at the time of the employee's retirement. As such, the investment performance is crucial to the amount of pension secured – a good investment performance is essential.

There can be problems here, because the Inland Revenue imposes the same benefit limits on company schemes operating on a money purchase basis as for final salary schemes, although it is possible for the accrued fund to acquire a pension above the Revenue limits if contributions have been high and the investment performance good. This is of particular relevance to executive pension arrangements where executives can and do pay a high level of contribution.

Pensions for Individuals

Personal pensions, which are pensions arranged by individuals, both employed and self-employed, have to be arranged through a life company, a bank, a building society or a unit trust management group, though there are facilities for investors to manage their own investments. Many banks, building societies and unit trust groups have their own life company subsidiary, and a personal pension contract from a bank, building society or unit trust group is often a contract issued by their life company.

There are two types of personal pensions: appropriate personal pensions used to contract-out of SERPS, and personal pensions, and both operate on the money purchase principle.

Appropriate Personal Pensions

Since appropriate personal pensions are used to contract-out of SERPS, the contributions and benefits must match those provided by SERPS. Employees, and their employers, who contract-out of SERPS get a rebate on their National Insurance contributions, amounting to 1.8 per cent for employees and 3.0 per cent for employers on the band earnings between the Lower and the Upper Earnings Limit. When an employee contracts-out of SERPS with an appropriate personal pension, this rebate of the combined 4.8 per cent of band earnings is invested in the contract by the DSS.

In addition, the employee gets basic-rate tax relief on his or her rebate. The 1.8 per cent is regarded as a net of tax rebate, so the gross rebate is 2.4 per cent. Thus a further 0.6 per cent of an employee's band earnings is invested in the contract. On top of these payments, the Government pays a further 1 per cent incentive contribution into all contract for individuals aged 30 and over, making a total of 6.4 per cent of an employee's band earnings paid over as a contribution to an appropriate personal pension, consisting of:

Employee's rebate	1.80%
Basic-rate tax on employee's rebate	0.57%
Employer's rebate	3.00%
	5.37%
Incentive contribution*	1.00%
Total contribution	6.37%

* For individuals aged 30 and over

The employee is not involved in the actual paying of these contributions, and just selects the life company for the appropriate personal pension contract.

The employer deducts the full National Insurance contributions and pays these to the Department of Social Security as normal. The DSS takes out the rebate and pays over both contributions, together with the basic-rate tax relief and the incentive contribution to the selected life company. However, the payment is not made until after the end of the tax year.

Thus, if an employee takes out an appropriate personal pension this year (1996/1997), the life company will receive the contribution a few weeks after the end of the tax year on 5 April 1997. This delay means that the contributions are not invested until the life company has received the contributions from the DSS.

The employee can have only one appropriate personal pension receiving contributions from the DSS at any one time. But he or she can switch their holdings from one life company to another.

Age Related Rebates

From 1997/1998 the system of rebates for contracting-out of SERPS will change for appropriate personal pensions (APPs) and company money purchase schemes (COMPs) from the present flat rate rebate system to a system where the rebate varies with the age of the individual. There will be slightly different rates at certain ages for APPs and COMPs to reflect the differences in timing as to when the contracts receive the contributions from the Department of Social Security.

The rebate on APPs will start at 3.4 per cent of band earnings for individuals aged 16 or below and rise to a maximum of 9 per cent for individuals aged 46 or over. For COMPs, the rebate varies from 3.1 per cent at age 15 to 9.0 per cent for individuals aged 47 and over. Tables 7 and 8 and show the full range of rebates.

However, the rebate for company final salary schemes remains on a fixed basis, being 4.8 per cent for 1996/1997 and 4.6 per cent for 1997/1998.

The implications of this change will be discussed later.

Table 7. Rebates for APPs 1997/1998 to 2001/2002

Age at beginning of financial year	% of band earnings
15–16	3.4
17–18	3.5
19–20	3.6
21–22	3.7
23–24	3.8
25–26	3.9
27–28	4.0
29	4.1
30–31	4.2
32–33	4.3
34	4.4
35	4.5
36	4.7
37	4.9
38	5.0
39	5.2
40	5.4
41	5.6
42	6.0
43	6.7
44	7.4
·45	8.2
46–63	9.0

Table 8. Rebates for COMPs 1997/1998 to 2001/2002

Age at beginning of financial year	% of band earnings
15	3.1
16–17	3.2
18–19	3.3
20–21	3.4
22–23	3.5
24–25	3.6
26	3.7
27–28	3.8
29–30	3.9
31–32	4.0
33	4.1
34	4.2
35	4.3
36	4.5
37	4.6
38	4.8
39	5.0
40	5.2
41	5.4
42	5.8
43	6.4
44	7.2
45	8.0
46	8.9
47–63	9.0

Investments

The employee has a complete choice of investments for the contributions on an appropriate personal pension.

Benefits

Since appropriate personal pensions are replacing SERPS, the benefits are payable at the same time as SERPS would be paid, at State pension age. The whole of the accumulated cash and the contract(s) must be used to buy an annuity. There is no cash sum available, just as there is no cash sum with SERPS. The annuity can be bought from any life company, but there are certain basic requirements:

- It must be on a unisex basis with the annuity rates quoted by the life companies the same for men and women – a new development for life companies.
- It must be on a unistatus basis, that is, it must provide a 50 per cent pension to the employee's spouse on the death of the employee, even if the employee is single when he or she takes the annuity.
- The annuity must increase by 3 per cent a year, or by the rise in the Retail Price Index if less. The Government pays the balance of the SERPS benefits.

Personal Pensions

At this stage, Charlie Easy-Going becomes interested as well as the others, because, being self-employed, this is the only way he can save for retirement on a tax-efficient basis.

Personal pensions are comparatively straightforward in their operation.

Contributions

The maximum contributions that can be paid into a personal pension are based on a percentage of an individual's annual earnings, the percentage increasing with age at the beginning of the tax year – the current levels being:

Age	Percentage of net relevant earnings
Up to 35	17.5%
36–45	20.0%
46–50	25.0%
51–55	30.0%
56–60	35.0%
61–74	40.0%

The earnings on which contributions can be paid are subject to a ceiling – the Cap mentioned earlier, the current limit being £82,200. The self-employed pay contributions gross and reclaim the tax in their Schedule D assessment. Those who are employed pay their contributions net of basic-rate tax, the life company or other provider reclaiming the tax from the Inland Revenue. The individual has to claim higher-rate tax relief from his or her local tax office through an adjustment in the tax coding.

Contributions can be paid as single premiums, with the individual reassessing his contribution each year, or as regular premiums. Many life companies have a recurring single premium facility that enables an individual to reassess and vary his contributions each year while at the same time ensuring continuity of payment.

Types of Contract and Investments

Individuals have a wide choice of contracts and investment funds from life companies and other pension providers, from deposit funds to esoteric equity funds.

DEPOSIT FUNDS

These funds are offered by a few building societies and banks and operate in a similar manner to ordinary deposit accounts. The individual pays his contributions into a special deposit account and interest is regularly credited on the accumulated value. The interest is paid gross and the individual cannot withdraw cash from the account, except to transfer it to another personal or other pension arrangement. The charges made by the bank or building society are either in the form of lower interest rates or a deduction from the contributions together with a slight reduction in the interest rates.

UNIT-LINKED FUNDS

These funds are offered by all life companies and those unit trust groups marketing personal pensions direct rather than through a subsidiary life company. The contributions, after deducting the initial expenses, are invested through buying units in the selected funds. Life companies offer a complete range of funds in which the individual can choose to invest his contributions:

- Cash funds
- Gilt and fixed-interest funds
- A variety of general and specialist UK equity funds
- A variety of overseas equity funds
- Property funds
- Managed funds – a mixture of the various asset classes managed by the life company
- Guaranteed funds.

All funds, except the cash funds, have two unit prices – the offer price and the bid price. The offer price represents the cost to the life company or unit trust buying the underlying assets, and this is the price which the individual pays to buy units. The lower bid price reflects the cost of releasing the assets and managing the fund, and is the value which the individual receives when he or she sells the units. The difference between the bid and offer prices, known as the spread in the price, is normally around 5 to 6 per cent, but can be higher.

With a unit-linked personal pension, the purchaser builds up a holding of units at the offer price, which, when he or she takes the benefits, are cashed in at the bid price. The price of units will depend on both general stockmarket and economic conditions, and the particular effects on the individual assets which make up the fund. Although over the long term unit prices should generally rise, there can be falls in the unit price, some dramatic, over shorter periods, particularly with equity and property funds. This is known as volatility, or investment risk, which the individual has to carry when he takes out a unit-linked personal pension.

This volatility can be avoided by investing in guaranteed funds, which offer a high return when equity markets are buoyant, but guarantee that the funds will not fall in value over the selected investment period. A more detailed description of the operation of these funds is given in chapter four.

The individual can split his contributions between as many funds as he desires, and between as many life companies as he wishes. He can switch between funds within a life company on favourable terms. He can switch his funds between life companies, but this can be expensive.

CONVENTIONAL WITH-PROFITS FUNDS

These funds are available from traditional life companies, which have been established for decades, if not centuries. They represent a mid-way house between deposits and the unit-linked funds, combining the higher returns available from equity investment with the stability of deposit cash funds. There are several variations on the with-profits theme, but the general mode of operation is as follows:

- Contributions from all individuals holding with-profit pension contracts are invested in a common fund, comprising the whole range of investments, but with equities and property dominating.
- The contributions made by each individual accumulate each year in two forms:
  - They increase from a guaranteed growth rate, usually at a low level.
  - They increase from a bonus rate declared each year by the life company from the profits of the underlying fund. The actuary smooths out the violent market fluctuations in the value of the underlying assets when determining the bonus rates. The combined growth rate is applied to the current value of the accumulated contributions, which means the accumulated fund grows in value over time, but at a rate depending on the profits achieved by the underlying funds. So although bonus rates can fall, and have fallen, the accumulated fund never falls in value. It is the rate of growth of the fund that varies.
- When the individual comes to take his benefits the accumulated fund is given a final boost from the application of a terminal bonus. This bonus reflects the movement in capital values of the underlying assets and tends to be more volatile than the annual bonus declarations.

Charges are not specific under a with-profits contract. The life company recoups its expenses from the common fund. The return on with-profits should, over the long term, outperform those from a deposit investment.

Benefits

The benefits of personal pensions include:

- The individual can take the benefits on a personal pension contract at any time between his or her 50th and 75th birthday, both dates inclusive.
- He or she does not have to cease working and retire in order to take the benefits, nor have to take the benefits because he or she has stopped work. There is complete flexibility as to when the benefits are taken.
- Up to 25 per cent of the accumulated value can be taken as a tax-free cash sum.
- After taking any tax-free cash sum, the individual then has a choice with using the remaining value. Either he or she buys an annuity straightaway with that value, or cash is withdrawn each year from the contract and an annuity bought at a later date. The annuity can be bought from any life company – it does not have to be bought from the life company which managed the personal pension.
- There are few restrictions or requirements as to the type of annuity bought with the money.
- If the individual dies before taking any benefits on his or her personal pension contract, then a death benefit is payable to the estate, normally free of inheritance tax. For most contracts, the benefit is the accumulated value of the fund at the time of death. But on certain with-profits contracts, the death benefit is a return of the premiums paid with interest.
- There is no limit on the benefits secured by a personal pension contract. The Cap only limits the contributions.

4

INVESTMENTS, PENSION PROVIDERS AND CHARGES

At the mention of investments, most people's eyes start to sparkle, for investments represent the glamorous side of pensions. To make the most suitable choice one needs a working knowledge of the various types of investment available on pension contracts as well as information about the different providers and their charges.

Generally, there are three alternative means of investing the contributions made to a pension arrangement.

Managing One's Own Investments

It is possible for an individual to manage his or her own fund, particularly with personal and executive pension arrangements, either directly or through an appointed investment manager, with the life company providing the administration services only. But few life companies or financial institutions offer this Do-It-Yourself investment service, and those that do offer the facility require a high minimum contribution.

Anyone taking this investment route should either be au fait with investments or have his own personal investment adviser/manager, such as a stockbroker. Even so, such investors need to consider their decision very carefully before committing themselves.

David Short-Sighted is interested in exploring the possibilities of handling his own investments and this will be discussed in dealing with David's pension arrangements. But the others agree that such involvement is beyond their capabilities.

Leave it All to the Life Company

This is the course of action taken by the vast majority of people in their pension arrangements, as most people feel that Do-It-Yourself investment is a risky business requiring a lot of expertise, or else cannot be bothered to take the trouble. They can either have a unit-linked arrangement and invest in the mixed or managed fund, or invest in the with-profits fund. In either case, the life company makes all the investment decisions.

The Middle Course

The third alternative represents a halfway house for individuals who want some involvement with the investment of their contributions without being swamped by the day-to-day investment decisions.

Life companies, in their unit-linked pension plans, offer a wide range of funds covering the main asset classes. The individuals choose the funds in which they wish to invest their contributions, while the life company selects and manages the investments within each fund. Individuals have the opportunity of spreading their contributions between various funds and switching their holdings between funds, including switching into the managed or with-profit funds. There is ample opportunity for them to be involved in the investment process if they desire.

Before considering particular investment funds, the investor needs to think about some general points. The pension received will depend on the value of the fund accumulated under the personal pension or other pension arrangement, so he or she needs to build up as large a fund as possible, seeking investments that offer the highest return. Ideally, the build-up in the fund should at least match the growth in an individual's earnings. If, for example, Charlie Easy-Going is paying a contribution of 10 per cent of his current earnings, then this should be invested so that when he retires it will have grown to at least 10 per cent of his earnings at retirement.

Rate of Return

An investor holding a portfolio of assets achieves growth on those assets in two forms:

- Income in the form of interest payments, dividend payments and rents.
- The rise in the capital value of the underlying assets, such as the increase in equity prices or property values. Capital growth can be negative.

The capital value of some assets, such as deposits, does not change.

So if over a year the dividend payment is 6 per cent and the capital value rises by 10 per cent, the rate of return is around 16 per cent (the precise calculation of the return is more complicated). If the capital value had fallen 10 per cent, the rate of return would be about minus 4 per cent.

Real Rate of Return

In pensions literature there is the expression 'a real rate of return', and an understanding of the meaning of this term is vital in selecting investments.

The real rate of return on an investment is simply the actual rate, less the rate of inflation: if the investment return is 12 per cent a year and the inflation rate is 10 per cent in the same year, then the real rate of return is 2 per cent for that year. A positive real rate of return means that the asset is increasing in value relative to inflation, and such assets will enable Charlie Easy-Going to maintain the value of his contributions.

However, the real rate of return on an investment can be negative, which means that its value, relative to inflation, is falling. If individuals invest in assets that show a negative real rate of return, then effectively the contributions are worth less at retirement than when they were made and Charlie's contribution of 10 per cent of earnings will, at retirement, be less than 10 per cent of his earnings at that time.

Stability and Investment Risk

Investors in pension contracts want as stable a fund as possible, with little variation in value – in technical terms, they want minimum volatility or investment risk. Some asset classes, particularly equities, and to a lesser extent property investments, have fluctuations in value over short periods – and this is the investment risk. If the investor takes the pension benefits at the time when the value of the fund is falling then he or she will receive a smaller pension; hence the need for stability.

Unfortunately, the investments offering the highest returns also have the greatest investment risk or volatility. When selecting the investments for the pension contributions an investor has to decide how much risk he or she is prepared to take in order to secure an adequate fund at retirement. Many people try to avoid making this decision by leaving everything to the life company, but it should be remembered that this does not completely remove the volatility in the build-up of the pension savings.

The range of assets in which individuals can invest their contributions are:

- Cash and deposits
- Fixed-interest stocks and bonds
- UK equities
- Overseas equities
- Property
- Guaranteed funds

Within each of these major categories, there are a host of sub-categories, particularly with UK and overseas equities.

Performance

Table 9 shows the average returns on a variety of investment classes over the last ten years.

Deposit and Cash Funds

Deposit and cash funds are the most easily understood of the investments available for pension contracts since most people have savings in bank and/or building society deposits.

The only differences between ordinary deposits and those used for pension contracts are that interest is credited gross instead of net, and an individual cannot make withdrawals, although money can be transferred to another pension investment. The money, like all other pension funds, is locked away from the investor until the conditions are fulfilled for the pension benefits to be taken.

The investment return on a deposit arises solely from the interest credited periodically on the value of the fund; there is no capital variation. The fund grows steadily in value with each contribution payment and each interest credit. As such the fund is stable with no volatility. The interest payments made are closely linked to the current general interest rates in the economy, and therefore interest rates on these deposits will vary just as interest rates vary on ordinary deposit accounts.

Cash funds from life companies operate in a slightly different manner. The investor buys units in a cash fund which has a single price generally guaranteed not to fall in value. The life company invests the fund in a variety of money market investments, seeking the best return.

Table 9 shows that cash funds achieved a steady return of 9.35 per cent a year over the past ten years, with a real return of nearly 5 per cent a year over the Retail Price Index.

Table 9. Average annual investment returns on pension funds

Year	UK Equities %	International Equities %	UK Property %	Gilt & Fixed Interest %	Cash Fund %	Mixed Fund %
1986	29.71	34.91	12.34	12.85	10.93	24.42
1987	14.18	−13.68	15.53	14.40	10.10	6.66
1988	8.97	15.94	24.94	8.59	9.41	12.63
1989	24.64	34.74	13.94	7.75	12.34	24.66
1990	−13.71	−23.68	− 6.75	3.67	14.21	−10.57
1991	14.11	18.69	0.32	15.81	11.60	13.84
1992	18.52	21.11	2.01	18.60	9.43	18.59
1993	27.92	34.79	17.18	22.93	5.47	29.69
1994	− 6.40	− 4.60	9.66	− 7.75	4.65	− 5.54
1995	20.52	15.75	2.06	15.32	5.79	17.08
Average Annual Return						
5 years 1986–90	11.66	6.78	11.50	9.38	11.38	10.75
5 years 1991–95	14.31	16.43	6.06	12.43	7.35	14.13
10 years 1986–95	12.98	11.50	8.74	10.90	9.35	12.43
Retail Price Index 10 years 1986–95			4.6% pa			
National Average Earnings 10 years 1986–95			6.5% pa			

Source: Micropal/Central Statistics Office

Since most investors feel very comfortable with deposit accounts, they may well be tempted to invest their pension contributions in these accounts on the assumption that they will meet their requirements and provide them with an adequate pension. Conditions during the ten-year period under review were good for deposits as interest rates remained high, but now that inflation has come down and is expected to stay down, then the returns could be much lower.

Although past investment performance is not an infallible guide to future performance, it can provide certain pointers as to what can happen. The table shows that cash funds had the lowest return but one of all investments over the past ten years, although almost the highest over the five years 1986–1990. Studies over longer periods going back several decades show that, except for certain very short periods, cash has been one of the worst performers in investment terms and there have been long periods, such as in the 1970s, when it failed to match inflation.

An individual will be investing the pension contributions for many years, and so must take a long-term view. A financial adviser would only recommend investment in cash and deposits over very short periods.

Fixed-Interest or Bond Funds

These funds invest in a whole range of fixed-interest stock, mainly in the UK. The most common and well known of these stocks is issued by the British Government, invariably referred to as gilt-edged stock or gilts, reflecting the absolute security in payment of interest and repayment of capital.

There are a variety of other fixed-interest stocks issued by local authorities, companies and corporate bodies, where security of payment may not be absolute. These funds may also include fixed-interest stock issued by foreign Governments and overseas companies.

The usual format for a fixed-interest stock is as follows:

- The stock is issued for a fixed period.
- Over this period, interest payments of a fixed, pre-determined amount – the nominal rate – are paid at regular intervals, often half-yearly.
- At the end of the period, the stock is redeemed by the payment of a fixed, pre-determined capital sum.

The main variation to this format is undated stock, where there is no fixed period and the stock is redeemed at the option of the Government or other body which issued the stock.

These stocks are transferable and the price paid for fixed-interest stock will depend on current interest-rate levels and the usual market forces of supply and demand. When interest rates rise, the prices of fixed-interest stocks fall, the size of the fall depending on the term to redemption and the nominal interest rate on the stock. Conversely, when interest rates fall, prices of fixed-interest stock rise.

An investor in a fixed-interest stock receives his return in two ways – the pre-determined interest payments and the capital gain (or loss) when the stock is sold or redeemed over the price paid for the stock.

The fixed-interest market is highly sophisticated and best left to the experts. But as Table 9 shows, even the experts cannot completely overcome the inherent weakness of fixed-interest stock – the payments may lose their value against inflation. Fixed-interest funds over the past ten years showed an average annual return of 10.90 per cent, only slightly better than cash. And a scrutiny of the fixed-interest returns for each year shows that these funds can be volatile.

It may therefore not be advisable to put contributions into a fixed-interest fund, with the possible exception of index-linked gilts, which are briefly described below.

Index-Linked Gilts

These are special British Government stocks where the interest payments and the capital repayment are revalued in line with the rise in the Retail Price Index, thereby maintaining their value in real terms measured against inflation. Thus these stocks provide investors with security of payments and a guaranteed real rate of return. But the supply of index-linked gilts is limited, and this means that the price of the stock is high and the overall returns low in relation to other funds.

Most professional fund managers feel that the price asked for the inflation guarantee is too high.

UK Equities

Many ordinary people participated in the various privatisation issues that have taken place over the past few years and may have made a healthy profit on these equities. But it should be remembered that the Government invariably issued the privatisation stock at too low a price, so that when the stock came on the market it was traded at a far higher price than the issue price, and those who received stock were able to sell at a useful profit.

There is no inbuilt low price for those equity stocks already on the market; one does not always make money on equities.

Privatisation has introduced the public to the concept of buying ordinary or equity shares. When someone, whether an individual or a financial institution, buys ordinary shares in a company, he or she becomes part-owner in that company and is entitled to share in the profits. The profits that are distributed are paid out in the form of dividends. Those holding ordinary shares can expect to receive a stream of dividends each year that should rise over the long term as profits rise; they are investing in real assets. In general dividends can be expected to rise, although dividend cuts can and do occur, even to the extent that companies may not pay a dividend if trading conditions are bad, although dividends may be paid out of reserves if profits are insufficient or losses are made.

Dividends represent the first part of the investment return on ordinary shares. Ordinary shares are traded on the stockmarket and the capital changes, the variation in the price of a particular stock over a period, say a year – the capital gain or loss – represent the second element in the overall investment return on an equity.

The overall return on equities consists therefore of two items, dividend payments and capital changes, both of which are subject to considerable volatility. Clearly there is a need for investors in ordinary shares to have a spread of holdings in different companies across the range available, to reduce the volatility of equity investment.

Over the past decades, most dividends have shown steady growth. The volatility in equity returns has arisen from the changes in capital values as represented by the share prices. As equity dividends rise, the underlying share prices should also rise. But share prices are affected by a host of factors – interest rates, economic conditions and outlook, and, above all, investor attitudes. Share prices can soar ahead of dividend growth and can also fall dramatically even though dividends are still increasing – the events in 1987 culminating in the stockmarket collapse on 19 October were a extreme example of just how volatile equity markets can be.

This volatility should not turn investors against equities, as the returns in Table 9 show that despite very poor returns in 1990 and 1994, which were negative, UK equities still achieved the highest annual return over the past ten years compared with other investments. Investors in equities must take a long-term view and keep a steady nerve, and they should regard a low, bear stockmarket as buying more equity units with their contributions.

The UK equity market is a complex affair and professional management is essential. This management and the required spread of investments is achieved automatically by investing in the funds managed by life companies and unit trust groups.

There can be problems with equity investment, particularly if an individual wishes to take the benefits when the stockmarket is depressed and the value of his pension contract has fallen, as was the situation in 1990 and 1994. The answer is not to reject equities as long-term investments but to be prepared to switch out of equities into more stable investments, such as cash or with-profits, two or three years before taking the benefits.

The lessons to be learned about equity investment are:

- It is investment in real assets offering the best prospects for long-term growth.
- Investors need to spread investments and obtain professional investment management, using a pooled fund.
- They must be prepared to switch out of equities as the time approaches to take their pension benefits.

Overseas Equities

Investment in overseas equities on a large scale has only been possible in the past decade or so, following the removal of exchange controls early in the Thatcher era of Government. On the principle that 'The grass is always greener on the other side of the fence', UK investors flocked overseas, investing billions. However, there are several points to bear in mind about overseas investment.

There are a variety of overseas markets for the investor to choose – the classic ones being the US and North American market, the Japanese and the Far Eastern markets and Europe – each with its own characteristics. The public, when investing in overseas markets, have tended to follow the current fashion, often lured on by high-powered advertising. First it was the US market, then it was Japan, then it was Europe. Results never really matched the 'hype' on the whole.

There is an additional factor when investing overseas – the currency risk. A UK investor first converts sterling into the local currency to buy the equity. Then when he cashes-in the equity he converts back from local currency into sterling.

The return to a UK investor on an overseas equity depends first on the dividends received, secondly on the share price movements over the period of the investment and finally on the exchange rate at the time of selling compared with the rate at the time of buying. In many instances, the excellent returns achieved from overseas equities have arisen as much from currency appreciation as from the rise in the stockmarket.

Overseas equities tend to be even more volatile than UK equities, dividend payments tend to be smaller, overseas stock-markets tend to fluctuate more than the UK market, and there is the additional currency factor. The need for a spread of professionally-managed equities is paramount for overseas investments.

The main justification for investing in overseas equities is the belief that they will, over the long term, achieve a higher return than investment in UK equities. But Table 9 shows that, while there have been some excellent years for overseas equity investment over the past ten years, they have not quite matched the returns on UK equities.

Investors have the choice of either investing in one or more particular markets, or investing in an international fund covering a variety of markets where the investment manager decides on which markets to invest in as well as selecting the particular stocks within a market.

Investors should not be warned off overseas investment completely but they should invest, at most, only a small part of their contributions overseas, and pick an international fund rather than a specific market. Above all, these investors must be prepared to switch out of their overseas investments near the time when they wish to take their benefits.

Property Investment

The public tend to have an inherent inclination towards investing in 'bricks and mortar', believing property investment to be both solid and safe. The events of the past five years, in relation to stagnating and falling house prices, have brought home to many people that property, as an investment, can get overpriced and that property values can fall as well as rise.

Life company and pension fund investment in property tends to concentrate on holding the freehold in prime office blocks, shops and industrial sites, buying into existing buildings and being involved in property developments. They tend to invest in the larger units. They do not invest to any large extent in domestic houses, though they can invest in luxury flats; neither do they invest in small units or the more speculative property holdings. In the past, they have invested in agricultural land and woodlands, but have tended to reduce such investments in recent years.

The return on the investment comes in the first place from the rents received. Rents on commercial and industrial property tend to be reviewed every three or five years and it is usual for rents to be increased at these reviews in line with the growth in the economy. However, properties can stand empty, producing no rents at all, particularly in times of depression.

Property investments, like equities, benefit from rises in the underlying capital values of the properties. While such values usually rise in line with rental growth, they are subject to other factors, and values can fall.

Property investment tends to be less volatile than equity investment. But Table 9 shows that property as an investment has not fared as well as other investments over the past ten years, with a negative return in 1990. It has, however, outperformed inflation.

Life companies and unit trusts offer these funds on a unitised basis. The individual selects the fund(s) in which he or she wishes to invest their contributions and buys units in the fund(s); when the investor wishes to take the benefits, he or she simply cashes-in the units.

The decision now is to select the particular equity or other fund from the large number of funds available to investors; the choice of life company is closely connected with this decision.

The vast majority of people taking out pension contracts leave everything to the life company. There are two sorts of fund – a mixed or managed unit-linked fund, and a with-profits fund.

Mixed or Managed Unit-linked Funds

This type of fund is promoted under both names – mixed because the underlying portfolio is a mix of equities, property, fixed-interest and cash, and managed because the life company's investment managers manage and vary the underlying mix of assets to obtain the optimum return.

The majority of the portfolio will be composed of UK equities, with a substantial holding of overseas equities. These funds now contain a far lower proportion of property and fixed-interest assets than, say, two decades ago. The funds operate on a unitised basis as described above. The long-term success of the professionals is shown in Table 9, where the average return over the past ten years easily outperformed inflation and earning growth over the period.

However, the managers cannot be expected to outperform every other asset over the long term. The returns on the property and fixed-interest content will dilute the equity returns. Indeed, the managers will always have to have some regard for limiting the fall in value of the fund when stockmarket conditions are adverse. As seen from Table 9, the returns on mixed funds can be negative, which means that the unit price will fall under these conditions, and hence individuals investing in mixed funds will still need to switch into cash funds when they approach the time to take their benefits. The funds are too large for the managers to switch into cash and anyway this would be detrimental to other unit-holders still some years from taking their benefits.

Individuals have to choose which mixed fund, a decision closely tied in with the choice of life company.

With-profits Funds

To achieve the maximum pension in retirement, funds should be invested for a high return, that is in equities. But as already stated, equity funds are quite volatile, that is their underlying values fluctuate quite dramatically although the long-term trend is upwards. Hence many investors are wary about investing heavily in equities.

There are two methods of circumventing this problem. The classic method is the with-profit fund concept, devised at Equitable Life over 200 years ago and followed by other traditional life companies. The other method, formulated literally over the past three or four years and still being developed, is Guaranteed Funds.

Despite the length of time that with-profits contracts have been available to investors, they are still barely understood by the majority of people. The with-profits system operates on a pooled basis, with the contributions, after deducting the initial expenses, being put into a common fund which invests in a mixture of equities, property and fixed-interest assets. The profits from this fund and the other business transacted by the life company are ascertained each year by the life company's appointed actuary following his valuation of the company's assets and liabilities. The directors of the company, on the advice of the actuary, determine how much of the profit should be distributed and the form in which it is distributed.

Mutual life companies with no shareholders distribute all the profits to the with-profits policy holders in the form of bonuses. Proprietary companies divide the profits between policy holders and shareholders, who receive their payment in cash as dividend payments. But policy holders in proprietary companies must receive at least 90 per cent of the profits from the with-profits fund.

There are as many types of bonus system as there are traditional life companies, but the general format for pension contracts is as follows:

- There is a low guaranteed growth rate on the contracts. This would probably be a growth rate in the region of 3.5 per cent a year.
- An annual bonus is declared and added to the guaranteed benefits on the contract; the bonus, once it has been paid, is itself guaranteed. These annual bonuses tend to be stable in amount from year to year.
- A bonus is either added when the contract matures or vests and the benefits are taken, or added to the annual bonus but not guaranteed. These final or terminal bonuses tend to be more volatile than the annual bonuses, being related to the changes in the capital values of the assets.

This is illustrated in the following example.

A with-profits pension contract with the company grows in value from year to year until the benefits are taken. The company declares a bonus and fund growth rate for a calendar year, but that bonus is not added (the technical term is 'vests') until the following 1 April. This makes the system somewhat hard to follow and many traditional life companies vest their bonuses immediately they are declared.

(1) A single investment of £10,000 was made on 31 December 1992.

(2) The initial expense deduction is 4.5 per cent – the costs of setting up the scheme – so £9,550 is invested and this is the initial guaranteed value.

(3) Guaranteed fund on 1 April 1993 = £9,550 × (1 + [91/365 × 0.035]) = £9,632, and on 31 December 1993 = £9,550 × 1.035 = £9,884.

(4) Declaration at 31 December 1993:
Bonus rate 4.0 per cent
Overall growth rate 13 per cent
These will apply on 1 April 1994.

(5) The total fund value on 31 December 1993 will be the initial value of £9,550 increased by 10 per cent, that is £9,550 × 1.13 = £10,792.

(6) The total fund value on 1 April 1994 will be the value in (5) increased by the interim growth rate of 13 per cent a year, that is £10,792 × [1 + (91/365 × 0.13)] = £11,141.

The fund value represents the total growth of the investment.

(7) The guaranteed value on 1 April 1994 is the value in (3) increased by one-quarter of a year's interest at 3.5 per cent a year = £9,632 × 1.035 = £9,970.

(8) Declared bonus added at 1 April 1994 is 4.0 per cent of the guaranteed value in (7) brought forward to the date, that is, £9,970 × 0.04 = £399 and the new guaranteed value = £9,970 + £399 = £10,369.

(9) The 1994 bonus statement would be:

	£
Guaranteed fund on 1 April 1993 b/f	9,632
Guaranteed interest and declared bonus	737
New guaranteed fund 1 April 1994	10,369
Final bonus addition	692
Total fund value 1 April 1994	11,061

(10) This process is repeated for 1994, when the declaration was:
Bonus rate 4.0 per cent
Overall growth rate 10 per cent.

(11) The 1995 bonus statement would be:

	£
Guaranteed fund on 1 April 1994 b/f	10,369
Guaranteed interest and declared bonus	777
New guaranteed fund 1 April 1995	11,146
Final bonus addition	1,021
Total fund value 1 April 1995	12,167

(12) This is repeated for 1995, when the rate was the same as for 1994. On 1 April 1996, the guaranteed value would have risen to £12,079 and the fund value to £13,386.

(13) The contract is cashed-in on 1 April 1996 and the benefits taken. The individual would receive the fund value of £13,386, and the guaranteed value acted solely as a safety net. The total fund value would never fall below the guaranteed value; that could only happen if the company declared a negative growth value, because investment returns had been disastrous.

Tables 10 and 11 show how this investment grew.

Table 10. Growth in a with-profit personal pension contract
Single investment of £10,000 made on 31 December 1992
Benefits taken 1 April 1996

Date	Guaranteed Fund b/f £	Interest £	Bonus £	Guaranteed Fund £	Final Bonus £	Total fund value £
31 Dec 1992	—	—	—	9,550	—	—
1 Apr 1993	9,550	82	—	9,632	—	—
1 Apr 1994	9,632	337	400	10,369	692	11,061
1 Apr 1995	10,369	363	414	11,146	1,021	12,167
1 Apr 1996	11,146	390	543	12,079	1,307	13,386

Unitised With-profits Funds

A new and growing concept is the unitised with-profits method of investment.

The investor buys units, after which charges are deducted. These units increase in value on a low guaranteed basis plus annual bonus declarations, and the unit value is guaranteed never to fall.

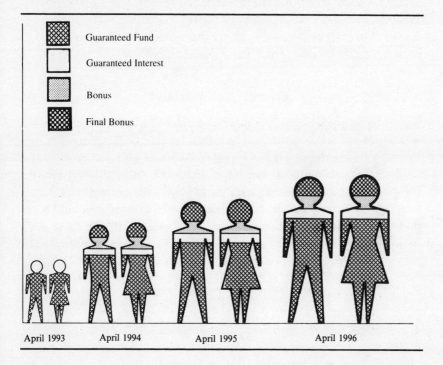

Guaranteed Fund

Guaranteed Interest

Bonus

Final Bonus

April 1993   April 1994   April 1995   April 1996

Guaranteed Funds

These funds offer investors the opportunity of receiving the high returns on their funds when the UK equity market is buoyant, but also guarantee that the funds will lose nothing or very little when the UK equity market is dull. This is achieved, not by investing in UK equities, but by investing in a combination of derivatives (Options and Futures) based on the UK equity stock market indices, which provide the equity growth and fixed-interest stocks, such as zero coupon bonds, which provide the no loss guarantees.

There is now a whole range of such guaranteed funds offering investors a wide variety of guarantees and returns, some of the funds offering very sophisticated benefits and guarantees.

Investors are still wary of derivative based products – still regarding them as highly speculative, particularly following the collapse of the long established merchant bank Barings. By themselves, derivatives are speculative. But when they are combined with other assets, the resulting products provide security with good returns. The derivatives market is well controlled by the London International Financial Futures Exchange (LIFFE) and life companies offering guaranteed products dealing only with well run merchant banks with great financial strength.

Overall Comparison

Table 12 shows how individuals would have fared over the past ten years having their pension contracts invested in different assets through funds managed by Equitable Life.

The UK equity fund outperformed most other unit funds, but the performance of the international fund was exceptional.

Individuals leaving all the decisions to the company would have done well with the managed fund. But they would have done even better with the company's with-profits fund, which outperformed every other fund except the International Fund.

Choice of Life Company

The choice of life company is an extremely difficult decision to make, as much depends on which adviser individuals use to help arrange their pension contracts. If investors use an adviser who represents just one life company, usually referred to as 'tied agents' by the media, then that representative can only recommend the contracts of the life company he or she represents. But if they use an independent financial adviser, then that adviser has a legal obligation, under the 1986 Financial Services Act, to recommend those life companies and contracts which will best meet the clients' requirements.

In any event, the investor needs to look at the life company being recommended to ensure that he or she will get good value for their money, and there are five main features which our characters and other individuals should check when looking at life companies:

- Sound financial basis with adequate capital resources.
- Good administration systems and service.
- Good investment record and ongoing investment team.
- Low charging structure.
- Forward-looking attitude by top management and staff.

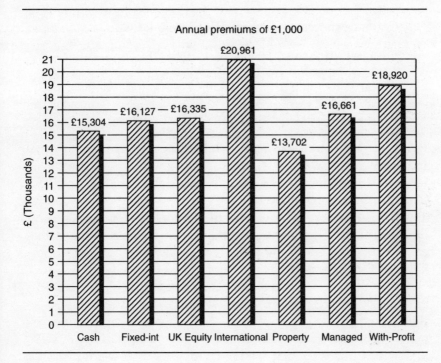

Annual premiums of £1,000

£20,961

£18,920

£16,127 — £16,335

£15,304

£16,661

£13,702

£ (Thousands)

Cash   Fixed-int   UK Equity   International   Property   Managed   With-Profit

With-profits Guide

Information on some of these points is provided by traditional life companies in their with-profits guide, which, under the financial service requirements, all companies offering with-profits contracts have to produce and make available to the public.

The with-profits guide gives information on:

- The company's bonus policy.
- Investment distribution in its with-profits fund.
- Solvency margins/Financial strength.
- Expense charges.
- Investment returns achieved by policy holders on maturing or vesting contracts.

The information may not be easily digestible and some calculations with a pocket calculator might be required before the figures can be fully understood.

Individuals should be looking for companies with:

- a high proportion of assets in equities, but not too much dependence on overseas equities;
- charges, which are shown as a reduction in yield, that do not exceed 3.5 per cent for ten-year pension contracts and 1.5 per cent for 25 years.

In this respect the charges of Equitable Life of 1.4 per cent for ten years and 0.8 per cent for 25 years are the lowest among traditional life companies; Standard Life's comparable charges are 3.3 per cent and 1.2 per cent respectively.

Many advisers rely heavily on the performance tables to assess life companies. These tables are published regularly in magazines and periodicals, and show which companies had the best performance for various funds.

Those interested in taking out pension contracts have access to a plethora of statistical information on past performance, so much so that there is a danger of utter confusion when using past performance tables to select a life company.

The investor is seeking the life company which will do best for him or her in the future and, as all the tables warn 'Past performance is no guarantee of future performance', the tables are not an infallible guide to selecting the life company which will give the best performance in the future.

Nevertheless, properly used, this information can be of help:

- Look at performance over long periods – at least five years.
- Look for consistency in performance over several years.
- Look at companies in the top six or seven places when comparing consistency, and not just the company in the top position.

The investor should then check out the other factors listed above, looking for low costs of setting up the fund, and a strong financial base.

Following this procedure will allow an investor to select a company likely to provide a good return on his or her money. But it will be a matter of luck whether at the end of the day it turns out to be the best return.

Many individuals will be recommended a life company by an adviser, and they should not be afraid to question that adviser as to why he or she is recommending that company, and to go through the factors listed above. Do not accept any recommendation at face value.

5

Lℒℒℒℒℒℒℒ

WHAT THE SELF-EMPLOYED CAN DO

Self-employed Charlie Easy-Going has at last been convinced of the need to save towards his retirement. So what does he do? The initial decision for Charlie to make is easy because there is only one option; if he wants to save in a tax-efficient manner, then he can only do so through a personal pension.

But now he is faced with a number of choices:

- How much should he pay each year into a personal pension?
- How should he invest the contributions?
- Which life company or other provider should he select for his personal pension contract?

Charlie should review these decisions each year until the time arrives to take the benefits. Then he has to decide:

- How much tax-free cash does he take?
- What type of annuity does he buy?
- Which life company does he select for the annuity?

How Much to Contribute?

Here the Inland Revenue sets out the maximum contribution which the self-employed can make each year to qualify for tax relief. The amount relates to an individual's age at the beginning of the tax year and is set out in Table 13 overleaf:

Table 13

Age	Percentage of Net Relevant Earnings
Up to 35	17.5%
36–45	20.0%
46–50	25.0%
51–55	30.0%
56–60	35.0%
61–74	40.0%

However, there is a ceiling imposed on the amount of net relevant earnings to which these contributions apply. This ceiling, known as the earnings Cap, was introduced in the 1989 Budget at a level of £60,000. It is usually increased each year in line with the rise in the Retail Price Index, and for the current financial year is £82,200.

Charlie's earnings in the current year will be £100,000, so he will be affected by the earnings Cap. The maximum contribution he can make in 1996/97 is 20 per cent of £82,200, that is £16,440. However, to his delight, Charlie discovers that although he pays over the £16,440 to the pension provider, his tax bill is reduced, since the contributions qualify for income tax relief at his top rate of 40 per cent. The actual cost to his pocket is therefore £9,864.

Charlie's junior colleague, Prudence Fairplay, aged 30, earns £25,000 so only pays basic-rate tax. She is living up to her name and starting early to provide for her retirement. The maximum contribution she can make is 17.5 per cent of £25,000: £4,375, on which she gets tax relief at 24 per cent, a net cost of £3,325.

Charlie, having decided to save towards retirement, was somewhat confused over personal pensions when he enquired how his brother-in-law, Archibald Foresite, also aged 45, had saved for his retirement. Archie has been saving towards his retirement for several years, following the example of his father, Terence Foresite, who has saved for his retirement ever since the 1956 Finance Act introduced pension plans for the self-employed. Archie's pension plans from a life company are called Retirement Annuity Contracts (RACs), the old style personal pensions.

Retirement annuity contracts ceased when personal pensions were introduced in July 1988. However, existing holders of RACs were allowed to keep their contracts in operation and to continue paying contributions on them. The holders of RACs can transfer the contracts into personal pensions, but the switch cannot be reversed. There are several differences between RACs and personal pensions, one important one being that, although the contribution rates are generally lower, the earnings Cap does not apply to RACs.

Archie Foresite is also earning £100,000. His maximum contribution this year is 17.5 per cent of £100,000, that is £17,500, compared with the maximum contribution of £16,440 which Charlie can pay.

Carry-forward Provisions

Charlie had his chance to take out an RAC, but left the decision too late. However, all is not lost in respect of his earnings of the past few years. Any individual eligible for a personal pension over the previous six years is able to carry forward any shortfall in contributions and pay it as a lump sum into a personal pension. There is only one proviso: the individual must pay the maximum contribution in the current tax year before using up any contribution shortfall in the previous six years.

Charlie has been self-employed for most of his life, certainly for the past six years. He can sweep up the contributions he would have paid as follows, remembering that the contributions for a particular year will be calculated on the rules for that year, not the current rules.

Table 14

Financial Year	Relevant Earnings* £	Contribution Rate %	Maximum Contribution £	Contribution Paid £	Unused Contributions £
1990/91	64,800	17.5	11,340	Nil	11,340
1991/92	71,400	17.5	12,495	Nil	12,495
1992/93	75,000	17.5	13,125	Nil	13,125
1993/94	75,000	17.5	13,125	Nil	13,125
1994/95	76,800	20.0	15,360	Nil	15,360
1995/96	78,600	20.0	15,720	Nil	15,720
					81,165

* Net Relevant Earnings limited by the Cap.

Charlie can receive the full benefit of the carry-forward provisions, amounting to £81,165, since he is just starting on a personal pension plan. The Inland Revenue provisions apply to anyone who did not pay the maximum contribution in the tax year, as seen by the following example relating to Prudence Fairplay. She became a partner in July 1993 and therefore is eligible for a personal pension as a self-employed person. But she was unable to pay the maximum contributions in 1993/1994, 1994/1995 and 1995/1996. The carry-forward provisions in her case are as follows:

Table 15

Financial Year	Net Relevant Earnings £	Contribution Rate %	Maximum Contribution £	Contribution Paid £	Unused Contributions £
1993/4	15,000	17.5	2,625	1,000	1,625
1994/5	18,000	17.5	3,150	2,000	1,150
1995/6	20,000	17.5	3,500	2,500	1,000
					3,775

How do Charlie and Prudence make use of these carry-forward unused contributions? They have several alternatives available to them, depending on their current financial resources. Under the Inland Revenue rules an individual, having used the maximum current contribution, then has to start at the furthest year back and work through the unused contributions.

So in Charlie's case, he would start with the £11,340 unused contribution for 1990/91 and work through each successive year as far as he is prepared to go. Prudence can also take a similar route, but can afford to wait a year or two.

Carrying Back Contributions

There is another concession – the carry-back provision, under which individuals can elect that part or all of their contribution paid in one tax year is treated as if paid in the previous tax year. So contributions for the tax year ending 5 April 1996 can be treated as though they were paid in the tax year ending 5 April 1995 providing there is a shortfall in contributions paid in that year. He can carry back as much of the current year's contributions as desired up to the shortfall and there is no requirement for the individual to pay any contributions in the current year. The individual must make his decision to carry back such contributions within three months of the end of the tax year in which the contribution is paid.

The carry-back provision is particularly useful for people with variable earnings, as seen from the following example for someone with a maximum contribution rate of 17.5 per cent.

1994/1995
Earnings £40,000 – maximum contribution £7,000.
Contribution paid £3,500
Shortfall £3,500

1995/1996
Earnings £20,000 – maximum contribution £3,500

If he or she paid the £3,500 contribution in 1995/1996, they would only get basic tax relief at 25 per cent, that is, the net cost would be £2,625. But if he or she carries back the contribution to 1994/1995, making up the shortfall, the tax relief will be 40 per cent, a net cost of £2,100 and a saving of £525.

The carry-back provisions are also useful in a year when income tax rates have been reduced.

Archie used the carry-back provisions when income tax rates were reduced in 1988/1989 – the top rate being cut from 60 per cent to 40 per cent. He had not paid his maximum contribution in the previous year, so he was able to carry back the balance from 1988/1989 to the previous year and get tax relief at 60 per cent instead of 40 per cent.

The carry-forward and carry-back provisions provide the self-employed with flexibility in payment of their contributions into personal pensions – an important feature for those with variable earnings.

Benefits

A personal pension contract will provide the self-employed with a pension and a tax-free cash sum, or just a pension. But at the moment, neither Charlie nor Prudence are concerned with the ultimate benefits of buying the pension.

The flexibility of personal pensions enables those like Charlie to phase their retirement over a period of years from working full-time to varying part-time working to ceasing work, taking part of their pension at each phase of their retirement. In order to take advantage of this flexibility, Charlie will need several personal pension contracts which can be cashed-in individually, when needed, over a period of time. If the benefits are needed all at the same time because the individual has ceased work overnight, then all contracts can be cashed-in together.

But a self-employed person needs to consider protection for himself or herself and his or her family during the intervening period until the pension and cash benefits are taken.

Death Before Retirement

If the individual dies before taking the benefits, the death benefit under the contact is paid. Most deposit and unit-linked contracts pay out the accumulated value of the underlying fund into the individual's estate. But practice varies between traditional life companies on their with-profits contracts. Some companies pay out the value of the fund. Other companies pay a return of contributions, with interest, on the death of the individual. This amount is invariably less than the accumulated value of the fund, unless the investment performance has been abysmal, and the difference will widen with the passage of time.

In theory, the money not paid out on death is added to the profits, thereby boosting the bonuses paid to those who survive. In practice, it only makes a marginal difference.

Charlie, being a family man, is deeply concerned about the death benefit and wants a return-of-fund contract. Prudence, on the other hand, being single, is not overtly concerned about the death benefit. Nevertheless it is a point that an investor should take due account of when taking out a with-profits contract.

Charlie also needs to realise that should he die within a few years of starting a personal pension a death benefit of the value of the fund is unlikely to be sufficient to provide his wife and children with adequate money to look after themselves. He also needs to take out a life policy to provide further cover.

Sickness

If the self-employed (or employed) person falls sick and is unable to work for a prolonged period there will be a gap in the contributions paid. Most personal pension contracts offer the self-employed the option of waiving contributions, and in these circumstances this option should be taken.

CONTRIBUTIONS – HOW LARGE?

So far, Charlie and Prudence are aware of the maximum contributions they can make into a personal pension. But can either afford to pay the maximum? Very few self-employed make such high contributions until very late in their working lives. Usually, the contribution paid is what the self-employed person can afford, and pension payments are well down the list of priorities for expenditure.

Charlie feels that paying the maximum 20 per cent of his capped earnings is rather excessive. He was thinking of contributing 10 per cent of the capped earnings – £8,220 – this year and increasing his contributions by 5 per cent each year (higher than the present inflation rate) until age 65.

To get some indication of the benefits provided by this contribution level, Charlie obtained a benefit illustration from a life company, assuming payment of contributions as indicated, until he was 65. The illustration, prepared on the official basis, showed that if his contributions earned 12 per cent a year, he would accumulate a sum of £829,000 by age 65 and this would provide a pension of £5,340 a month (£64,080 a year) which would increase by 5 per cent a year and leave his widow with a half pension on his death.

Charlie was satisfied with these figures and questioned whether he could pay less into his personal pension. However, Charlie has ignored the future growth in his earnings. On the official illustration basis, if his contributions earned 12 per cent a year, he could expect his earnings to increase by 9 per cent each year. On this basis, Charlie would be earning around £860,000 a year at age 65, and the illustrated pension would be just over 7.4 per cent of those earnings.

The sad fact is that even if Charlie pays the maximum 20 per cent, he is not going to secure an adequate pension unless the investment performance is phenomenal. These figures again emphasise the message that delay means lower pensions.

The warning to all individuals seeking to secure an adequate pension is to check out what their contributions will secure, not just in money terms but as a percentage of their anticipated earnings at retirement. In this respect, the official illustrations are far from complete in providing that information.

Charlie has to decide whether to pay contributions regularly each year on a pre-determined basis, or assess each year what he should pay. Since Charlie has to assess his earnings annually anyway, it is logical that he should assess his pension contributions each year with single premiums, rather than make regular payments.

Investments

Charlie and Prudence have to decide on how to invest their contributions. Charlie's nature towards investment is somewhat of a paradox as, having taken risks in his business life which have paid off, he is reluctant to take any further risks with the money he is earning. To date he has kept his money on deposit, building up substantial sums. Secondly, Charlie is wary of following a course of action over which he has no control. He likes to be in charge, particularly if the event involves risk. Hence, he is very reluctant to hand over his money to a life company to follow an investment procedure involving risk over which he has little control.

Since cash and deposit funds have done well in the past, Charlie's immediate reaction was to invest with the same banking institution where he had his savings, this institution being one of the very few to offer a deposit fund for personal pensions. Charlie now realises that interest rates are lower and could come down even further, so he ought to look for a higher return over the long term than that offered by deposit funds.

Nevertheless, Charlie is right to look at the investment risk involved. He ought not to go to the other extreme and invest all his contributions in a high-risk fund seeking a high return. The best strategy for Charlie, and for most people, is to spread the risk. A possible strategy for Charlie could be as follows:

- Use the first part of his contributions to secure a firm foundation. A with-profits personal pension is ideal to provide this foundation. The contributions can be paid and Charlie can forget about the rest until the time comes to take his benefits. He decides to invest one-third of his contributions in a with-profits personal pension and maintain future contributions at this ratio.
- Now he can afford to be more adventurous with the remaining contributions. But Charlie's nature will not let him go overboard. So he agrees to invest a further one-half of his contributions in a general UK equity fund and

accepts that he will need to check on this part of his investment each year and be prepared to switch.

- With the final one-sixth of his contributions, Charlie decides to be adventurous and invest in an overseas equity fund – one which he is prepared to monitor and switch. Charlie is optimistic about the future of the European Community and Eastern Europe, so for a start he is investing in a European fund. But he expects to be either switching out of this fund or putting future contributions into another overseas fund.

Prudence, being rather cautious, has up to now been putting all her contributions into a with-profits personal pension. This is a sensible approach for someone with relatively low contributions, where it is not financially viable to split contributions. But now her earnings are rising, Prudence can afford to split her contributions between contracts. She has decided to maintain last year's contribution into the with-profits contract and invest the balance into a UK equity fund.

She will maintain this approach until the contributions are divided 50–50 between the with-profits and the equity contract and then keep this division of her contributions. When she nears retirement, she intends to switch out of the equity fund back into with-profits.

The permutations for investment are numerous. The overriding feature is that the individual should feel comfortable with his investments and be prepared to change as circumstances change.

Choosing the Life Company

Finally, Charlie has to select a life company or companies in which to make his investments for both the with-profit and the equity-linked personal pension contracts. He is not restricted to using one company. There are three major factors which Charlie needs to consider in selecting a life company: its investment potential; the charges made on its contracts; and its financial strength.

It is not easy to judge the investment potential of a life company. There are certain indicators which can help select companies with good investment potential – past record over the short and long term, its current investment team and strategy, and its portfolio composition. Essentially, Charlie should look for a company with a consistently good record over a long period – not necessarily a current top performer, but one rarely out of the top few companies. The past performance tables published by certain leading personal finance magazines are useful in making such selections.

It is easier to check on the charges made by a life company on its various contracts. The effect of charges on both with-profit and unit-linked contracts are shown in the product particulars which have to be supplied when contracts are being sold. But Charlie does not have to collect these illustrations in advance. The magazines mentioned above also publish tables of the illustrations using a common investment return – the companies with the highest illustrated returns have the lowest charges.

The financial strength of life companies is difficult to assess, even for professionals in this field. One needs to look at several factors – the ratio of assets to liabilities, the capital backing of a company, its mix of business. Again the magazines mentioned above produce articles assessing the financial strength of various life companies.

Charlie obtained the relevant copies of these magazines, looked at the relevant tables and selected two life companies – one for the with-profits contract and the other for the equity linked contract. Both had good investment records, low charges and adequate financial strength.

Prudence decided to invest the equity fund in the same life company in which she already has her with-profit contract. She is satisfied with the company's bonus record and investment record. And as already pointed out, it can be expensive to switch life companies in the early years.

6

PENSIONS FOR THE EMPLOYED

Peter Hard-Worker and Susan Briteyes plan their retirement savings.

Peter's employer, Forward Enterprises, runs a company scheme – FE Pensions – where membership is entirely voluntary. Peter now feels it is time to provide for his retirement, but is not quite certain how to proceed. He has two courses of action:

- join the company scheme, FE Pensions, and make any further provision on top of this scheme, or
- make his own arrangements through personal pensions.

Making the Decision

First of all Peter needs to get all the information possible on the company scheme and what help, if any, he can get from his employer if he wants to take out a personal pension. The company's pensions department is obliged, by law, to provide Peter with certain information on the scheme, but he found that, like in most companies, the pensions department was very willing to help.

The pensions department provided Peter with a statement showing the various benefits provided by the scheme, and the less welcome information that he would have to contribute 6 per cent of his pensionable salary to the scheme – another reason why Peter has done nothing up to now. But the pensions department pointed out how the blow to his pocket was softened by the tax relief available to him on these contributions.

Up to now, Peter was in SERPS and paying the full National Insurance contribution of 2 per cent of his earnings up to the Lower Earnings Limit and 10 per cent on the rest of his earnings up to the Upper Earnings Limit. If he joins FE Pensions, then because the

72

BENEFIT STATEMENT

FE PENSIONS

PERSONAL INFORMATION

Name HARD-WORKER P   Salary £40,000

Date of Birth 23 JULY 1953   Pensionable Pay £35,624

Normal Retirement Date   Date from which Pensionable Service
  23 JULY 2018   is calculated 23 JULY 1996

The benefits under the scheme are pay related and definitions vary for different purposes. The figures below are based upon information available on the date shown and should be taken as an indication only of your benefits. In particular retirement benefits will be based on pay at or near retirement.

BENEFITS ON DEATH BEFORE RETIREMENT

Lump Sum	£80,000
Pension Payable to Your Widow	£7,421 p.a.
Allowance Paid to Eligible Child	£2,474 p.a.

BENEFITS AT NORMAL RETIREMENT DATE

Your Pension	£14,843 p.a.
or Lump Sum	£37,500
and Reduced Pension	£9,693 p.a.

BENEFITS ON DEATH AFTER RETIREMENT

A Pension will be Payable to Your Widow	£7,421 p.a.

CONTRIBUTIONS ARE PAYABLE AT THE RATE OF 6%
OF PENSIONABLE EARNINGS

See Notes overleaf for further information

scheme is contracted-out of SERPS, Peter pays 1.8 per cent less on his National Insurance contributions on his band earnings between the Lower and Upper Earnings Limits. And he gets tax relief at his top rate of 40 per cent on the 6 per cent contribution to the company scheme. Thus his costs before and after joining the scheme would be:

Before:	£
Gross Earnings	40,000
less National Insurance contributions	2,112
less income tax	9,990
Take-home Pay	27,898

After:	£
Gross Earnings	40,000
less National Insurance contributions	1,743
less company pension contributions*	2,114
less income tax	9,143
Take-home Pay	27,000

*Gross Earnings	£40,000
less 1½ basic State pension	4,770
Pensionable earnings	£35,230
contribution = 6% of pensionable earnings =	£2,114

The reduction in Peter's annual take-home pay through joining the company scheme is £898 – just 3.2 per cent.

But Peter needed more information about the benefits under the scheme, in particular:

- What happens if he should fall ill and be unable to work?
- What happens if he retires before the normal retirement age of 65?
- What happens if he delays retirement after 65?
- What benefits would he get if he left the company?
- How have pensions been increased over the past few years and what is the company's policy on pension increases?

The answers Peter received from the pensions department were that the scheme:

- Provided full pensions on ill health retirement.
- Provided generous benefits on early retirement.
- Followed the normal practice of enhancing benefits for late retirement.
- Followed the normal practice of providing benefits for employees leaving the company.
- The company has a policy of increasing pensions, on a discretionary basis, as far as financial circumstances permit. Over the past ten years, pensions have been increased on average up to 75 per cent of the rise in the Retail Price Index over the period.

Peter next asked the pensions department the following questions about his employer's policy towards his taking out a personal pension outside the company's own scheme, and received the following answers:

- Will the company contribute towards a personal pension?
  Answer: Nothing beyond the statutory minimum for contracting-out of SERPS.
- Does the company still provide death-in-service benefits to employees not in the company pension scheme?
  Answer: Lower benefits would be paid of just once his salary for the lump sum benefit and half the normal pension benefits for his widow and children.

Seeking Advice

The pensions department could not give Peter more specific advice since, because of the uncertain legal position over the Financial Services Act, the company had adopted the common practice of not giving advice on personal pensions direct to its employees. However the company did have an arrangement with a firm of independent financial advisers to whom it could refer any employee seeking information on personal pensions.

Peter took advantage of this arrangement, but although the adviser explained personal pensions in detail there was no way of directly comparing the benefits provided by the company scheme with other personal pensions to see which offered Peter the better choice.

Making the Choice

The company's pensions department gave Peter a list, compiled by the National Association of Pension Funds, of questions employees should consider when choosing between company schemes and personal pensions.

1. *How old is the employee?*

The older the employee, the more advantageous is a company final salary scheme compared with a personal pension. Peter is almost 40 – the borderline age for this decision – so has no advantage either way.

2. *Is the employee likely to change jobs frequently?*

When an employee changes jobs, he usually suffers a reduction in accrued benefits on his company final salary scheme, whereas an employee takes his personal pension from job to job. As Peter feels that he is now settled in his present job, it will make little difference which scheme he chooses.

3. *How much will the employer contribute?*

The employer meets the balance of cost in his company scheme, but is not obliged to pay anything to a personal pension. Peter has ascertained that his employer will not contribute, and the independent adviser demonstrated that to achieve an adequate retirement income on a personal pension, Peter would have to contribute more than the 6 per cent he would contribute to the company scheme. So a company scheme is more advantageous.

4. *Who pays for the costs of running the pension scheme?*

Under a company scheme, the costs are met by the employer. With a personal pension, the life company deducts its costs and expenses either from the contributions or the underlying fund, or both. So a company scheme is cheaper in this respect.

5. *What happens if the employee is ill and unable to work?*

A company scheme usually provides generous pensions if the employee is forced to retire through ill health. His employer's scheme would provide a pension based on the number of years of his potential service to normal retirement, should Peter fall ill or become disabled and be unable to continue working.

With a personal pension, Peter would only receive the State benefits which, like State pensions, are low, plus whatever pension could be bought with the accumulated value of the personal pension; the accumulated value would be lower and the annuity rates lower, so the pension would be very much lower. The cost of taking out insurance to provide an income in the event of Peter falling ill has to be paid for by Peter on top of his pension contributions.

6. *What happens if the employee dies before retirement?*

Company schemes provide generous death-in-service benefits – a tax-free cash sum, spouse's pension and dependants' pension. With a personal pension, Peter's widow and children would get just the accumulated value of the personal pension plus the reduced benefits from the company of a lump sum of just once Peter's salary and half the normal pension benefits due to him. Peter would need to buy life cover, thereby reducing the contributions to the personal pension. For both death or illness before retirement, the company scheme is more advantageous.

7. *What happens if the employee retires early or delays retirement?*

A company scheme enables an employer to be generous on early retirement, whereas with a personal pension the employee has to suffer the full actuarial reduction. In contrast, the later the time of retirement the more advantageous the personal pension becomes.

Although Peter feels that he is settled in his present job, he has seen colleagues retire early and would not be averse to retiring himself a year or two early, whereas he would not really want to continue working after his retirement date. So again the company scheme offers Peter more.

8. *What happens to the spouse's pension on the death of the employee after he or she has retired?*

Company schemes pay a spouse's pension (now to widowers as well as widows) on the death of a pensioner in the company scheme up to two-thirds of the employee's own pension. With a personal pension, the employee has to buy a spouse's pension at retirement, thereby reducing the overall pension. Married employees get more benefit out of company schemes than single employees. Since Peter is married with a young family, the company scheme offers him far more value.

9. *Does the pension maintain its value against the eroding effects of inflation?*

By linking the pension to an employee's final salary, the build-up in pension automatically maintains its value against inflation. Once the pension starts, few schemes other than the public sector schemes automatically revalue the pension each year in line with the rise in the Retail Price Index. Most company schemes provide a low guaranteed pension increase – usually 3 per cent or 5 per cent a year – and pay further increases on top of the guarantee on a discretionary basis. From April 1997, schemes must revalue pensions accruing from that date in line with the RPI up to a maximum of 5 per cent a year. Peter's employer's scheme has a good record of such discretionary pension increases.

In contrast, with personal pensions, an employee has to pay for inflation proofing.

10. *What is the employee's temperament?*

Does the employee want to do his own thing? Is he prepared to spend a lot of time and effort each year arranging and revising his personal pension plan? If so, then the employee will take out a personal pension come what may and ignore all other arguments against personal pensions. But Peter, by his very nature, has been far too busy up to now to even think about pensions and it is unlikely that he would be prepared to devote much time in the future to looking after his own pension. Company pensions do not involve the employee in their operation; they are hassle-free, which fits in with Peter's temperament.

Since the answers to all the other questions were either in favour of the company scheme or neutral, it did not take Peter very long to select the company scheme.

However, he is joining his company scheme rather late. As seen from his benefit statement, his company pension at the normal pension age of 65 will only be 37.11 per cent of his salary (reducing to less than one-quarter if he takes the maximum cash sum), though he will also receive the State basic pension and some SERPS pension. Peter appreciates that he should have joined the company scheme earlier. Indeed very few employees, for one reason or another, qualify for a full two-thirds pension. Employees in company pension schemes should:

- Look carefully at their annual benefit statement, together with details of their State pension, and check on the amount of pension as a percentage of their earnings instead of throwing the statement away or losing it in a drawer.
- Consider whether that pension will be sufficient at retirement.
- If not, then consider taking action to boost that pension by paying extra contributions.

Peter has accepted the need to boost his benefits and is prepared to pay extra contributions. He made enquiries at the pensions department and found that the Inland Revenue would not permit him or any employee in a company pension scheme to take out a personal pension. However, Peter can pay extra contributions into an AVC (Additional Voluntary Contribution) arrangement – the equivalent of a personal pension in some respects, getting tax relief at his top rate of 40 per cent on those contributions. Again there are certain choices to make:

- How much can and should he contribute?
- Which AVC arrangement should he use for those extra contributions?

How Much to Contribute?

AVCs are considered by the Inland Revenue to be part of the company pension arrangement and thus come within the limits laid down by the Revenue. The effect of these limits on the contribution which Peter, or any other employee, can make to an AVC arrangement is twofold: there is a direct contribution limit, and there is an indirect benefit limit.

Employees can only pay a maximum contribution each year in to a company scheme of 15 per cent of earnings, including the contribution to the main company scheme. Thus Peter can pay a maximum annual contribution into the AVC as follows:

Total annual contribution =
15% of £40,000 (total earnings) =   £6,000
Annual contributions to the main scheme =
6% of £35,230 (pensionable earnings) =   £2,114

Maximum contributions to an AVC =   £3,886

The pension secured by the AVC, added to the pension provided by the main company scheme, must not exceed the Inland Revenue limits for a pension – usually two-thirds of earnings at retirement. Such a situation, known as overfunding, can arise in practice if the employee pays high contributions into the AVC and there is a good investment return on the underlying assets. The employee should check that the contribution he pays will not breach these limits. In practice, the AVC provider or the adviser will provide a check.

In Peter's case the exercise would be academic, as there is so much leeway to make up. And the amount of contribution paid is, like that of most employees, restrained by what he can afford.

Since most AVC arrangements operate on the money purchase principle, it will not be known for certain until retirement whether there is overfunding. In the past, if overfunding occurred it caused considerable problems since the Inland Revenue would make the company cut back the excess in the main company scheme. But now, any overfunding is paid back from the AVC arrangement as a cash sum, less an automatic tax deduction of 35 per cent for basic-rate taxpayers plus an additional higher rate charge for higher-rate taxpayers.

Peter decides to pay £50 a month – 1.5 per cent of his salary. He usually has the choice of paying £50 a month, in which case he needs to review his contribution each time his salary increases, or he can arrange to pay 1.5 per cent of his salary, in which case his payment to the AVC will automatically rise with each rise in his salary.

Which AVC Arrangement?

Peter has a choice of two AVC arrangements in which to pay his extra pension contributions:

- The in-house scheme operated by the company pension scheme; all occupational schemes must have an AVC facility to offer their members.
- A free-standing AVC from a life company.

It is not an either/or choice for Peter. Employees can invest in both the in-house and a free-standing AVC, provided the combined contribution does not exceed the official limits. But to invest in both on an efficient basis would, in practice, require the employee to be making substantial AVC contributions. Although Peter thinks that £50 a month is a lot out of his earnings, he accepts that it is not large enough to split between the two types of AVC and that he must decide on one of them.

Before making the choice, Peter needs to understand how each operates, what they offer and what charges are made. The main features can be summarised as follows:

	In-house AVC	**Free-standing AVC**
Benefits	Usually operates on a money purchase basis with the accumulated fund buying an annuity at retirement. Public sector schemes and a few company schemes offer an alternative final salary 'added years' basis.	Operates on a money purchase basis.
Contributions	Deducted automatically from salary with tax relief credited immediately.	Paid net of basic-rate tax by direct debit, but higher-rate tax has to be reclaimed by the employee.
Investments	The available investment funds may be restricted.	A wide range of funds is available – equity, mixed and with-profits.
Charges	Low.	The usual level of life company charges.

Considering charges first, the in-house scheme looks more attractive and there is less hassle in the payment of contributions and getting tax relief. Although most company pension schemes employ a life company or a building society to manage the in-house AVC scheme, the charges made by the life company are very much lower than on individual free-standing AVCs. For example, The Equitable Life, the largest provider of AVC arrangements to occupational pension schemes, makes an initial charge on each contribution on a sliding scale from 2.5 per cent for small schemes reducing progressively the larger the scheme, plus an annual management charge of 0.5 per cent. On its free-standing AVC schemes, the company makes an initial charge of 4.5 per cent on with-profit contracts and 5.0 per cent on unit-linked contracts –

with reductions for annual contributions of £5,000 or more – plus an annual management charge of 0.5 per cent.

A commission-paying life company could charge as much as 5 per cent initial and 1 per cent annual renewal, plus a policy charge of £2.50 a month on its free-standing AVC contracts. But the employee must check out that the lower charges are not at the expense of lower investment returns.

In-house AVCs

Many in-house AVC schemes offer employees a limited range of investments, compared with free-standing AVC contracts, and so the in-house scheme may only offer the choice between:

- Investment in a building society.
- A with-profits investment.
- Investment in either a building society or with-profits contract.

The rationale behind this lack of choice is generally that the in-house scheme wants to keep the administration to a minimum. So it offers the type of investment which the majority of employees want – invariably a straightforward, relatively risk-free, understandable investment such as building society deposits or with-profits. Such a restricted choice means that the pension department does not have the potential problem of being asked by employees which investment they should put their contributions into.

AVCs represent the final tier of an employee's pension provision, and as such the employee can afford to be more adventurous in investing his AVC contributions, taking a risk to secure a higher return without endangering his main pension. The more forward-looking pensions departments offer investment facilities to cater for those employees willing to take a risk as well as for those who still want a safe investment for their AVC contributions. For example the choice could be:

- Building society deposits.
- With-profits.
- A series of unit-linked funds, equity, property, fixed-interest and a range of UK and overseas equity funds, including a high risk Special Situations fund, and a mixed fund. The employee can spread his investments between these

choices and switch his fund from one investment to another.

Investment Advice

Employees should remember that the pensions department cannot do more than provide very general advice on the nature of each type of investment; it cannot give specific advice to individual employees on the investment of their contributions unless the department is authorised to do so under the 1986 Financial Services Act.

An employee arranging a free-standing AVC adviser can get that specific advice on where to invest his contributions. If the in-house AVC offers a wide range of funds, an employee should, on rational grounds, only take out a free-standing AVC because he considers that the life company managing the free-standing AVC can produce a better investment performance than the life company managing the in-house AVC which will more than offset the higher charges. But many employees like free-standing AVCs because they consider them to be their own contract and not the company's, a view fostered by many intermediaries selling free-standing AVCs.

Peter's company offers a complete investment package on its in-house AVC contract and, after investigating both types, Peter opted for the in-house scheme. He took the opportunity to be more adventurous in his investment, with the aim of getting a higher return and so a larger pension, by investing £30 a month in a general UK equity fund and £20 a month in a higher-risk overseas equity fund. Had the in-house AVC not offered equity investment, Peter would have gone for a free-standing AVC, despite the higher charges.

Peter knows that when his retirement is near, he should consider switching out of equities into deposit or with-profits.

The Inland Revenue generally requires all AVC contracts to be cashed-in and a pension bought on the day an employee retires, though it is possible to transfer a free-standing AVC into a personal pension. If retirement coincides with a depressed equity market, the employee will suffer if his investment is in equities, hence the need for Peter and other employees to consider switching out of equities at least a year or two before retirement.

Susan Briteyes' Position

Susan Briteyes has been taking note of the current trend of wives becoming more financially independent of their husbands, and, encouraged by her husband, decided to have her own pension. She is currently earning £16,000 a year, high enough to justify making her own arrangements.

Susan enquired about the company pension scheme and asked the same questions listed above. But her answers were rather different from Peter's. On question 1, Susan, aged 30, is young enough for personal pensions to offer better opportunities than the company scheme. Regarding question 2, Susan could well soon leave the company.

She looked at the other questions. The need for death and sickness benefits did not cut much ice with her, since her husband was not financially dependent on her. Nor was she worried at this stage about the problems with buying the pension. Her temperament was urging her to 'do her own thing' and she needed little persuasion to take the personal pension route to saving for retirement – savings which she could take with her if and when she left Forward Enterprises.

Contract-out or Stay in SERPS

Susan's first decision was whether to contract-out or remain in SERPS. Her choice to come out of SERPS and take out an appropriate personal pension was not a difficult one to make; employees in a similar situation to Susan should make the comparison between SERPS and an appropriate personal pension, taking a year at a time.

If Susan stays in SERPS in the year 1996/1997, she will pay the full National Insurance contribution, on which she does not get any tax relief, and qualify for one year's benefit – £54.95 a year in present money terms, an amount that is revalued in line with National Average Earnings. The amount of this benefit depends only on the employee's earnings and the year in which the employee reaches State pension age.

If she opts out of SERPS into an appropriate personal pension, she will automatically have 6.4 per cent of her band earnings paid into the contract, made up as follows:

Susan's NI rebate	1.80%
Tax relief on Susan's rebate	0.57%
Employer's NI rebate	3.00%
Incentive contribution	1.00%
Total contribution	6.57%

Susan's earnings of £16,000 are below the Upper Earnings Limit of £23,660, so her band earnings this year are £16,000 less the Lower Earnings Limit of £3,172, that is £12,828, and the contribution to the appropriate personal pension for this year will be 6.40 per cent of £12,828, that is £821. Payment of this contribution is automatic and Susan does not have to pay contributions to the life company. She and her employer pay the full National Insurance contribution, and the Department of Social Security and the life company handle everything else.

As was mentioned in chapter three, the National Insurance rebate is changing to an age-related system from April 1997. The combined rebate for Susan, then aged 31, for 1997/98 will be 4.2 per cent – slightly lower than the present rebate. What are the implications?

An age-related rebate reflects the actual cost of replicating the SERPs benefit for each individual for those years in the age band, rather than being a global average figure for all individuals, as previously. Thus age will no longer be an important factor in deciding whether or not to contract-out of SERPS.

The factors to consider will now be:

- Whether the expenses charged by the life company are lower than the expense figure used by the Government Actuary in calculating the rebate levels.
- Whether the returns which the life company can achieve on its investment funds will exceed the average investment return assumed by the Government Actuary in his calculations.
- Whether the individual is prepared to accept the investment risk inherent in a personal pension in the expectation of a higher pension or prefers the guaranteed benefit offered by SERPs.
- The actual earnings of the individual. Contracting-out is not usually beneficial for an individual on low earnings just above the Lower Earnings Limit.

These factors mean that in deciding what to do, the individual should check the expense levels and the investment record of life companies. Equitable Life, for example, has a good investment record and is renowned for having one of the lowest expense levels among life companies.

Now Susan has to decide in which fund to invest her contribution and select the life company for the contract. Some life companies offer a wide range of linked funds for investment in their appropriate personal pension as well as for their personal pensions. Other companies, however, take the view that the appropriate personal pension is replacing the guaranteed SERPS benefit and therefore the underlying fund should not be too risky, so they offer only a with-profits fund. Susan accepts this viewpoint and opts to invest her contributions in a with-profits fund. So she selects a traditional life company with a good record of results and low charges.

Personal Pensions

Now Susan considers making further savings for her retirement by taking out a personal pension in addition to the contracted-out appropriate personal pension, and now has to make decisions, similar to those already faced by Charlie Easy-Going, on how much to contribute, where to invest the contributions and how to select the life company/companies.

The contribution limits are exactly the same for employed persons as for the self-employed. So Susan can contribute a maximum of 17.5 per cent of her earnings, that is £2,800 a year, or £233.33 a month. She gets full tax relief on these contributions. But unlike the self-employed, Susan would pay the contributions to the life company net of basic-rate tax so she gets the tax relief automatically, the life company reclaiming the tax from the Inland Revenue. Employees in the higher tax bracket reclaim higher-rate tax from the Inland Revenue, usually by an adjustment in their tax code.

To determine how much she can afford, Susan should do some arithmetic. Her take-home pay after income tax and National Insurance contributions is:

	£
Gross Earnings	16,000
less National Insurance	1,346
less income tax	2,780
Take-home Pay	11,874 a year
	989 a month

Susan's monthly expenses are approximately:

Contribution to mortgage	150
Contribution to housekeeping	230
Clothes	250
Fares	90
Other	150
	870

So Susan feels she can pay £100 a month gross – net cost to her is £76 a month – into a personal pension. Should she pay single or monthly premiums? For self-employed Charlie Easy-Going it was preferable for him to pay the contributions as a single payment each year. But the employed are in a different position than the self-employed over the timing of paying contributions. Payment has to come out of their income and they do not have an annual assessment each year to ascertain their earning and their tax liability as do the self-employed. For the employed, paying monthly in step with their salary payments is usually easier than accumulating money to pay by single premium. But those wishing to pay by monthly premiums should check if the life company charges extra for this facility.

Investments

Next Susan has to select the investments and the life companies. Since she has 20 years to go before the first date on which she can draw the benefits – at age 50 – and longer for her expected retirement, she has time to adopt an adventurous approach in her investments with the aim of building up her pension savings funds to as high a level as possible, and to consider switching to less risky investments, such as cash or with-profits, when she is within a few years of retirement.

In addition, Susan has started to take an interest in investments generally and is prepared to actively look after her holdings in the personal pension contract. So she is in a position to invest in equity funds that need to be closely monitored and switched if conditions change. She decided to start off by investing half her contributions (£50 a month) in a UK equity fund and half (£50 a month) in an overseas equity fund.

If Susan had not been prepared to take an active role in looking after her investments, but simply wanted to pay over the contributions and forget about everything else, then she should invest in either the mixed fund or a with-profits fund and leave all decisions to the life companies.

Choice of Life Company

Her final decision is the choice of life companies. Susan does not have to put all her personal pension contributions with one life company, and neither does she have to select the same life company as she chose for her appropriate personal pension, though that company may offer a contract that, by combining the two personal pensions, can reduce the charges. Susan should concentrate on the company's investment record, not only for its experience in the selected equity fund, but look at the overall record in case she wants to switch funds. She also needs to check out the charges made by the life companies, although she should not select a company solely on its charges.

All that is left is to remind Peter and Susan to keep their pension arrangements up to date.

7

EXECUTIVE PENSIONS

David Short-sighted, a controlling director of a family business, has two alternative courses of action in saving for his retirement. He can either:

- Take out a personal pension, with his business paying the majority of his contributions, or
- Take out an executive pension arrangement – technically a company pension arrangement – for just himself.

In either case, David, being 50 years old, should remain in SERPS, and build his pension arrangement on top of SERPS.

Because he is starting his pension arrangements rather late, his over-riding concern is to build up as big a pension as possible. This in turn means paying the maximum contribution into the pension arrangement.

Both the personal pension and the executive pension arrangements operate on the money purchase system. So, since the underlying investments in either arrangement are the same, the value of the fund in each arrangement at the time the benefits are taken will depend on the contributions paid into each arrangement.

David and his company can pay 25 per cent of his earnings into a personal pension and 30 per cent next year when David will be 51. Since he is earning £100,000, his contributions into a personal pension are limited by the ceiling of £82,200. So David could pay a maximum contribution of £20,550 this year, rising to £24,660 next year, if the ceiling limit remains unchanged, plus any carry-forward amounts.

But David and his company could pay far larger contributions into an executive pension arrangement. Executive pension arrangements are company pension arrangements for one or more directors or executives, but the number of members rarely exceeds double figures.

As it is a company scheme, David's business – Long & Short Limited – as the employer, must pay contributions into the scheme. In fact, the business will pay the bulk, if not all, of the contributions. An executive pension arrangement is a flexible and tax-efficient way of transferring assets from the business to provide for David's retirement. It ensures that the business will provide for David's retirement, without causing problems for David's son, Kevin, when he takes over running the business. However, an executive pension arrangement is more complex than a personal pension. Being a company scheme, it has to be set up under trust, though David himself would most likely be one of the trustees. David has three choices available to him in setting up his executive pension arrangement:

- He can take out a pension contract with a life company.
- He can operate his own scheme – known as a Small Self-Administered Scheme or SSAS.
- He can have a hybrid arrangement that combines certain features of a life company scheme with an SSAS.

A straightforward executive pension contract with a life company is appropriate for providing top-up benefits to executives and senior personnel in major companies.

Running Your Own Scheme

For controlling directors and executives in family businesses and unquoted companies, an SSAS or a hybrid may be more appropriate. The directors who are being provided with pensions would be the trustees of the scheme and, as such, would be responsible for running the scheme, including managing the investment policy, although the Inland Revenue insists that there must be an independent trustee on the board of trustees, known as a 'pensioneer trustee'. People acting as pensioneer trustees have to be approved by the Inland Revenue. These trustees have certain defined responsibilities and powers conferred upon them. Essentially, the pensioneer trustee's task is to ensure that the scheme is well run and that the trust is not wound up by the members and the assets distributed between them.

Directors running an SSAS will need the help of advisers – an actuary, an administrator, an accountant and an investment adviser, as well as a pensions consultant to set up the scheme and provide on-going advice. Often one person or firm, including many life companies, offers several of these advisory services, including providing a person to be the pensioneer trustee.

The other feature resulting from an executive pension being technically a company pension arrangement is that the benefits are subject to Inland Revenue controls and limits, which in turn determine the maximum contributions that can be paid.

But being a money purchase scheme, the benefits at the time of retirement depend on the value of the fund built up. The Inland Revenue have agreed a basis whereby the actuary to the life company or consultant firm can determine the contributions that will provide the benefits. Since an actuary's assumptions are rarely, if ever, achieved in real life, what happens at the time of retirement will be considered later.

Benefits

The situation regarding the benefits is complicated because at present there are three different regimes in operation by the Inland Revenue, depending on when the scheme started and when the member joined.

Since David is starting from scratch, he will be controlled by the latest regime. But he will find that it is different from those operated by other companies which already have schemes.

Under a company pension arrangement, the maximum build-up in pension which the Inland Revenue will permit is 1/30th of earnings for each year of membership. So David can acquire a full pension of two-thirds of earnings in the minimum period of 20 years. This 20-year period relates to his time as an employee, not the membership of the scheme, and since David has worked for Long & Short Ltd since he left university, there are no problems for him achieving a maximum pension.

Since it is a company scheme, the Inland Revenue require the scheme to have a stated normal pension age, between ages 60 and 70.

David has not yet thought about when he will retire from the business, just that when he does retire he wants a pension that is paid separately from the business. So he obtains three quotations on the benefits for retirement at age 60, 65 and 70, and the corresponding contributions.

The maximum-level annual premiums which can be paid into an executive contract are:

Pension Age	Maximum Contributions £
60	120,000
65	76,359
70	52,635

David is married. If he were single, the maximum contributions would be lower, since he would not be funding a widow's pension. This confirms that he can pay up to as much as five times more contribution into an executive pension arrangement, thereby securing a far larger pension.

In fixing the pension age, David needs to make sure that he selects an age that qualifies for maximum benefits. David can select a pension age of 60, since he will have worked for his company for the minimum period of 20 years.

Death Benefits

Being a company scheme, an executive pension arrangement can provide death benefits of a cash lump sum, plus a spouse's pension should the director die before he retires, together with a return of contributions. The maximum cash sum permitted is the usual four times earnings up to the ceiling, in David's case £328,800. And the cost of funding these death benefits is treated as being on top of the contributions to provide the pension – in contrast to personal pensions.

The death benefits will be on a discretionary basis, so paid free of inheritance tax. This will help the business over the cost of meeting an inheritance tax liability should David die before retirement. The death benefits would be secured on a contract from a life company, irrespective of which type of executive arrangement is selected.

Buying the Pension

When the director wishes to retire and take a pension there are certain alternatives:

- If it is an executive pension contract for one person with a life company, then the fund is liquidated and an annuity bought in the usual manner.
- If it is an SSAS, there are two choices:
  - (a) either the annuity is bought straight away, or
  - (b) the scheme pays the pension to the director for the first five years and then an annuity is bought.

A full consideration of the implications of when to retire and buying the annuity is dealt with in the next chapter.

Overfunding

If the contributions into an executive pension scheme are high and the investment performance is good, there is a danger that at the retirement of a director the scheme is overfunded in that the benefits bought by the fund's value exceed the Inland Revenue limits.

This can be avoided in several ways, including increasing the salary of the director. But earnings will have to be averaged over at least three years, so it is necessary to plan ahead to avoid having to make a massive salary rise in the last year before retirement. So, directors need to constantly review their pension scheme with their advisers.

Contributions and Tax Relief

The life company or consultant determines the overall contribution rate to provide these benefits for David, who has to decide, first, whether he and the company can afford to pay the maximum contribution, and, secondly, how to split the contribution between himself and his business. Being a company scheme, the business is required to make contributions. However, the Inland Revenue permit a company to vary its contributions, within certain limits from year to year, into its pension arrangements to reflect the company's changes in profits.

Contributions into an executive pension arrangement can be considered in two parts – the regular annual contribution and a special contribution. If Long & Short Ltd has a good trading year it can afford to pay more into the executive pension arrangement, while in a poor year it wants to be able to pay less. The Inland

Revenue will accept a higher contribution, justified on actuarial considerations.

But if a higher contribution is paid because profits are high, then the Revenue may spread the additional contribution for tax relief purposes over two or three years depending on the size of the extra contribution relative to the regular contribution. Nevertheless, even if the tax relief on higher contributions is spread, the company will receive substantial tax mitigation in the year as well as in the following years.

The current rate of corporation tax is 33 per cent, but small companies with profits of £250,000 or less are charged a lower tax rate of 25 per cent. Companies earning between £250,000 and £1,250,000 get marginal relief, that is, they are taxed at 25 per cent on the first £250,000 and 35 per cent on the balance.

Long & Short earned pre-tax profits last year of £500,000. Without any pension contributions, its corporation tax liability would be:

$$
\begin{array}{rcl}
25\% \text{ of } £250,000 &=& £62,500 \\
35\% \text{ of } £250,000 &=& £87,500 \\
\hline
\text{Total} & & £150,000
\end{array}
$$

that is an overall rate of 30 per cent.

The after-tax profits are £350,000.

But if the company pays a contribution into a pension arrangement of £100,000, the pre-tax profits are reduced to £400,000 and its tax bill will be:

$$
\begin{array}{rcl}
25\% \text{ of } £250,000 &=& £62,500 \\
35\% \text{ of } £150,000 &=& 52,500 \\
\hline
\text{Total} & & £115,000
\end{array}
$$

and the after-tax profits will be £285,000.

Thus the net cost to the company of paying the £100,000 contribution is £350,000 minus £285,000 = £65,000, that is, the company has received tax relief at 35 per cent on the contribution. If the pre-tax profits had been just £250,000, then the tax relief on any contributions would be 25 per cent. If the pre-tax profits after making pension contributions were in excess of £1,250,000 the tax relief would be 33 per cent.

Investments and Costs

Now David has to decide on the form for his executive pension arrangement. But first of all, he is still concerned about possible financing problems with the business and the money being locked away in the pension scheme. Executive pension arrangements have special investment facilities, the first of which will ease David's concerns over finance.

Loans

Under all three pension arrangements, there are facilities for loans being made to the business from the pension scheme. But there are conditions:

- Such loans can only be made for genuine commercial reasons.
- The business must pay a commercial rate of interest on the loan – three points above the base rate is usually regarded by the Inland Revenue as a commercial rate.
- The loan must be repaid by the time the executive reaches normal pension age.
- The amount of the loan, plus the value of any shares in the company held by the scheme, must not exceed 25 per cent of the value of the pension arrangement in the first two years, and 50 per cent thereafter.

But providing these conditions are met, the loan is automatic, something that David regards as a plus point for pension arrangements. If his bank manager gets awkward, he has another source of finance available to his company.

Once a loan is made, it becomes an asset of the executive pension arrangement. The company will get tax relief on the interest and pay the interest net to the pension arrangement. The pension arrangement, being tax free, receives the interest gross, by reclaiming the tax from the Inland Revenue.

Differences occur between the three pension arrangements regarding property investment.

Property Investment

A major attraction of an executive pension arrangement to David and other controlling directors lies in its use to fund the purchase of property in a tax-efficient manner for use by the business, such as an office, factory or warehouse. Indeed, David has learned from talking to other directors that they originally set up their executive pension arrangement, usually an SSAS, for the sole purpose of a purchasing company property. This is done as follows, assuming the business wishes to purchase an office block for £250,000:

- The company pays contributions worth £250,000 into the pension arrangement. Since it gets corporation tax relief on these contributions, the net cost is £166,667, assuming the company pays corporation tax at 33 per cent.
- The pension arrangement buys the office block with the contributions and it becomes an asset of the pension fund.
- The fund leases the office block to the company at a commercial rent, which is reviewed periodically in the normal way. Assessment of the rent and the reviews must be made by an independent valuer who was not involved in the purchase or sale of the property.
- The company get corporation tax relief on the rent it pays to the pension fund. The fund itself receives the rent gross, by reclaiming the tax from the Revenue.

The Inland Revenue has never been completely satisfied with using an SSAS to buy property occupied by the parent company.

When the director wants to retire and draw a pension, the assets in the scheme have to be realised and an annuity bought. Property is not a readily realisable asset and there could be problems for the company trying to rearrange the financing of property which it occupies. The Inland Revenue therefore requires several years to elapse between buying the property and the director retiring. It is even better if there is more than one director in the scheme with a good spread of ages so that the scheme is on-going when the director concerned retires.

This facility to invest in a specific property may not be available on a straight executive pension contract from a life company. But it can be done through an SSAS. As a result, thousands of SSASs were set up with the sole purpose of buying property for company use.

The reaction of life companies was to offer directors a hybrid scheme, whereby at least 50 per cent of the assets must be invested within the funds offered by the life company, with the remainder being self-invested by the director as trustee. But David and any other director cannot use an executive pension arrangement to buy their own house or for any private residential property purchase; a pension mortgage is rather different and is dealt with later.

David appreciates that, with the facility of the pension arrangement to make loans back to the company and finance property purchases, it is far more tax efficient to build up funds in a pension arrangement for future company use than to build up such funds within the company. In addition, if an outside body did get control of Long & Short, that body could not touch the pension scheme assets.

Company Shares

An SSAS or a hybrid scheme has the facility to invest in the shares of the parent company, a useful facility to prevent unwanted persons acquiring shares in the company. However, it is no longer possible to buy shares from a connected person – that is, a relative or spouse or relative of a spouse. An SSAS can only acquire shares from third persons.

The Inland Revenue is understandably wary that such a facility may be abused as, since the shares are unquoted, there is no market on which to base the price. So the Inland Revenue requires that the price at which the shares are acquired is determined independently and that the pension scheme holds no more than 30 per cent of the equity and voting power.

Overall Investment

The general investment requirements of an executive pension arrangement are similar to those of other pension arrangements. Money not invested in one of the special investments already discussed can be invested in the complete range of assets for pension funds.

Like all money purchase schemes, when the director wishes to retire and take his benefits, then his fund has to be cashed in and an annuity bought. But, since for an SSAS the fund can pay the pension for the first five years before buying an annuity, time is available to organise the cash-in assets in an orderly manner.

Trading

Here a word of warning needs to be given to directors handling their own investments.

The tax-exempt privileges given to the investments of pension schemes only apply while the fund invests in what are regarded as normal assets.

The Inland Revenue takes a hard line against anyone abusing these privileges. It came down very heavily on one executive fund and on its consultant which it discovered buying and selling properties situated in its local area.

There is a particular problem with what are regarded as normal assets – equities and gilts – if the fund buys and sells its holdings in an excessive manner. The Inland Revenue could regard this as trading and subsequently tax the fund as traders. One part of the return on an investment is the rise in the price of an asset. Buying and selling stocks and shares can improve the return on the portfolio. The Inland Revenue accepts this aspect of portfolio management, providing the activity is not excessive. However, it refuses to define what it considers excessive.

It would become suspicious if the fund sold and bought back the same stock within 24 hours; it would be suspicious if the portfolio was completely revamped every month. But otherwise it is very difficult to know where the dividing line exists.

Directors doing their own investment, either themselves or through their stockbroker, should not take fright and keep assets that should be sold, thereby reducing the overall return on the portfolio. But they should keep a careful record of all transactions in case the Inland Revenue were to make enquiries.

Such problems are avoided if directors invest through funds managed by life companies or other financial institutions.

Investment Strategy

The investment choice and strategy adopted by the director or executive will depend first on his temperament and secondly on his business requirements.

Those directors not prepared or not interested in dealing with the investments, and with no foreseeable expansion plans, should keep with a life company executive pension contract, investing in a with-profits and/or managed fund. If they wish to be more adventurous, then they can invest in the equity fund and switch. They should pick a well run life company with a good investment record and low charges.

However, for directors like David, who like to be involved and want to make use of the potential given by an executive scheme in helping run the business, an SSAS or a hybrid scheme could be more suitable.

David likes the idea of running his own scheme, though he admits that he has little knowledge of investments. He and his fellow directors are considering plans for extending the company's operations over the next decade. As such David is attracted to the facility to take loans from the pension scheme and to buy property, and he is comforted by the knowledge that if necessary he can keep control of the company in the family through the pension scheme being able to buy shares in the company. And he can see that the scheme can help ease any inheritance tax problems in transferring the business to his son.

So he has set up a hybrid scheme with a life company, with himself and his son Kevin as trustees and beneficiaries. In addition, he has taken out separate cover for the maximum death benefits.

Kevin is currently earning £50,000, so the maximum contribution which he can make to the scheme for retirement at age 60 is £42,949, or £32,669 at age 65. Kevin can select age 60, thereby increasing his contribution, without being concerned about the problems at retirement. By selecting this age, the combined maximum annual contribution for David and Kevin is over £110,000 – a payment that would give the scheme a good financial start.

A hybrid contract is essentially in two portions – that invested with the life company and that where the directors are responsible. The size of the split is at the discretion of the directors.

In the portion which the directors are responsible for, David and Kevin are investing in a cash fund with the life company for quick accessibility, should they need funds to implement their expansion plans. They are keeping two-thirds of the contributions in cash earmarked for future expansion.

However, they do not intend to let the cash build up into a large cash mountain as has happened in several other SSASs, where the directors keep the money on deposit because they have not thought further than using the scheme to reduce their tax bill.

Later on, depending on how matters develop, David and Kevin will invest money in other assets, primarily equities. But they will use funds managed by the life company. They do not have the expertise to do it themselves.

The other portion, starting at one-third of the contributions, is invested in funds managed by the life company – at this stage a spread of UK and overseas equity funds. But as the time nears for David to take the benefits, they will switch into with-profits.

The charges made by life companies and consultants to operate an SSAS and a hybrid are as varied as the number of players in this field; much depends on the underlying services provided.

Some consultants charge a flat fee per scheme plus a fee per member, or a percentage of the contribution. This structure results in high unit costs for comparatively low contributions, but much lower unit costs for the big contributions.

Others charge a percentage of contributions, usually in banded form, but again unit costs tend to be lower for large contributions.

David and any other controlling director setting up a pension arrangement should check out the charges and the services provided, just as they would check out any of their suppliers in running their business. Having set up a scheme, it can be costly to switch arrangements.

8

BUYING THE PENSION AND INVESTING THE CASH SUM

Buying the pension is the final and the most difficult series of decisions to make in saving for retirement; the standard of living for the investor and his or her family during retirement will depend on the outcome. The decisions taken now are irreversible, and there is no subsequent opportunity to alter them. So everybody must be fully aware of the choices available to them and the consequences of the various alternative decisions.

The Inland Revenue imposes certain rules and restrictions on taking a cash sum and buying an annuity from the accumulated savings, and the rules vary slightly for different categories of pension.

Andrew Foresite is the brother of Charlie Easy-Going's father-in-law, Terence Foresite. Andrew is a solicitor who, having reached age 65, is retiring from his practice. He has been saving for his retirement over many years through a series of retirement annuity contracts (RACs) and now has £300,000 available through them, the old-style personal pension contracts. As the new-style personal pensions were only introduced in July 1988 very few people will, as yet, be taking their benefits on these personal pensions. The vast majority of the self-employed now reaching retirement will have saved through RACs.

Andrew, like all self-employed people, on reaching retirement or in the years approaching retirement, has three major decisions:

- When to cash-in his contracts.
- How much of the benefits to take as a tax-free cash sum.
- What type of annuity to buy with the remaining value.

There is flexibility in taking the benefits on an RAC, and Andrew does not have to take the benefits simply because he has stopped work. He can cash them in at any time between ages 60 and 75 – not quite the same spread of ages as for the new-style personal pensions. Andrew has no other income beyond the basic State pension and this means that the decision as to whether to cash in the contracts now and buy a pension or to defer cashing-in is effectively taken for him: he and his wife need income now and that can only come from cashing-in all his RACs.

Andrew now considers his next decision – how much of the benefits he should take as tax-free cash.

Cash or Pension?

First of all he needs to know how much cash he can take and how much pension would be left. The rules for calculating the maximum amount of cash that can be taken from an RAC are complex, compared to the new-style personal pensions, where up to 25 per cent of the value can be taken as cash.

The maximum cash that can be taken on an RAC must not exceed three times the single life annuity secured by the remaining value of the contract. If A is the amount of annuity per unit, then the proportion of the value of the contract that can be taken in cash is $3A/(1+3A)$. The greater the size of A, the annuity rate, the greater the proportion of the contract that can be taken in cash.

Annuity rates increase with the age of the individual at the time of buying the annuity, and the longer he or she can defer taking the benefits on an RAC, the greater the proportion that can be taken in cash. This is one reason why those already holding RACs are keeping them in force and not transferring the benefits to a personal pension; the other main reason is that the contributions are not limited by the ceiling on earnings.

RAC annuity rates are lower for women than for men of the same age, and women can take out less in cash from their RAC than men.

To get the maximum cash sum, the individual needs to buy the annuity from the life company with the highest rates, but except in certain circumstances this cannot be done at present.

Since RACs are no longer available, an individual with an RAC wishing to secure the pension from another life company would have to transfer to that company's personal pension scheme to buy that pension. This would mean that the cash sum would be limited to 25 per cent of the value of the RAC.

The exception would be if the individual also has an existing RAC with the life company with which he or she wishes to secure the annuity. In such a case, it may be possible to transfer the other RACs to that existing RAC contract, thereby retaining the more favourable treatment in calculating the cash sum.

So to get maximum cash from his RAC, Andrew has to buy his annuity from the life company which issued the contract and to which he has been paying contributions.

The proportions under Equitable Life's current annuity rates for men are 25.3 per cent at age 60, 27.6 per cent at age 65, 30.6 per cent for age 70 and 34.4 per cent for age 75. These proportions illustrate how much more tax-free cash can be taken from an RAC compared with the 25 per cent from a personal pension.

The decision on whether to take the cash and, if so, how much, has to be made at the time of taking the benefits; it cannot be deferred. If no decision is taken, the complete value must be used to buy a pension.

The natural tendency of most people when offered this choice is to take the cash rather than the income. Many have already decided how to spend the money – a holiday home, a new car, a world cruise – and it is unlikely that they will ever have the opportunity again to receive such a large cash sum.

If the person is in poor health, then the cash should be taken without much thought; why will become apparent when considering the decision of buying the annuity.

Andrew has no plans for spending the money. He and his wife need the income. Even so, on balance he should take the cash sum for these reasons:

- If he uses all the value of the contract to buy a pension, that pension is taxed as earned income.

    But if he takes the maximum cash and buys a similar type of annuity, that annuity is taxed less harshly – a concession from the Inland Revenue. The result is a higher net income for Andrew and his wife.
- The pension is one family asset that cannot be passed on to the next generation. Once Andrew and his wife have died, all pension payments cease and their children receive nothing. However, if Andrew takes the cash, it can be invested in a bond or a unit trust or even a building society account. Andrew and his wife receive the income,

admittedly less than from an annuity, but the capital can be passed on to their children.

● With the advent of independent taxation, Andrew can gift the cash sum to his wife and she can invest it to provide herself with an income, either by buying an annuity or investing in a bond, unit trust or building society to pass on the capital to the children. Or, since annuity rates increase with age, Andrew's wife can invest the cash and buy an annuity later.

However, one should not take the cash automatically and then just leave it in the bank on the grounds that 'cold cash gives me a warm feeling'. The decision should be carefully considered and everyone should plan how they intend to use the cash before they receive it.

Buying the Pension

We have referred to people taking the value of their pension contract and securing a pension by buying an annuity from a life company, without explaining fully what an annuity is.

The expression incorporates a whole range of contracts whereby an individual, on the payment of a pre-determined cash sum, receives in exchange a series of regular payments, usually until he or she dies, when the payments cease. The life company carries the mortality risk, making the payments irrespective of how long the annuitant lives. But there are numerous variations on this theme.

When an individual uses the cash value of the pension contract to buy an annuity, he or she secures a series of payments at regular intervals from the life company, and those payments provide him or her with a pension for the rest of their lives. There is no fear of the money running out before he or she dies, as there is when someone lives on their ordinary savings in retirement.

Andrew has had his RACs with Equitable Life. When he enquired about buying an annuity he was bewildered by the choice available.

There are five main categories of annuity:

● Level payments.
● Payments which increase each year at a pre-determined rate.
● With-profits annuities, where payments increase each year according to the bonus declarations.

- Unit-linked annuities, where payments are linked to the unit value of an underlying fund.
- Index-linked annuities, where payments are linked to rises in the Retail Price Index.

If this was not confusing enough, Andrew found there were even more complicated variations. He could:

- Have an annuity on just his own life, so that when he died the annuity payments stop.
- Have an annuity on the lives of himself and his wife, so that if he died first, payments continued to his wife until she died. Andrew would have the choice of continuing those payments at the same rate, or at a pre-determined reduced rate. He could even reduce payments to himself if his wife died first.
- He could have the annuity payments guaranteed for a fixed period and if he was still living at the end of the period those payments continued until he died. For example, he could have the annuity payments guaranteed for five years and then continue for the rest of his life. He could also have the payments guaranteed for a period on an annuity on himself and his wife.

The Inland Revenue have only two major restrictions on using an RAC to buy an annuity:

- The guaranteed payments period mentioned above must not exceed ten years.
- Where a spouse's pension or other last survivor annuity is taken out, the annuity paid to the spouse must not exceed that payable when both persons were alive.

Otherwise, there is complete freedom and flexibility over the choice of annuity. There is no limit on the amount of annuity purchased or the rate of increase in annuity payments.

Ideally, Andrew wanted an annuity that gave him the highest possible starting income, where the payments kept their real value against inflation and continued until both he and his wife were dead. But such pensions are only available to civil servants and other employees in the public sector when they retire. Andrew has to buy his pension with his own, not taxpayers' money, and the higher the annuity the more it will cost him.

He discovered that the annuity that gave him the highest starting income did not provide any protection against inflation. The annuity that protected him against inflation started at a much lower value. If he wanted an annuity for himself and his wife then the annuity payments were even lower. And if he wants those payments to be guaranteed then the payments are lower still.

Table 16

Pension annuity bought with £100,000 cash – Man aged 65		
Monthly	Year	Reduction in starting income
£	£	%
Single Life		
Level annuity 952	11,424	—
Annuity increasing by		
3% a year 758	9,096	−20.4
5% a year 640	7,680	−32.8
10% a year 390	4,680	−59.0
With-profits annuity		
Anticipating 3.5% growth 692	8,304	−27.3
Anticipating 7.64% growth 936	11,232	− 1.7
Index-linked 663	7,956	−30.4
Joint Lives – Man aged 65, Wife aged 62		
Level annuity 842	10,104	—
Annuity increasing by		
3% a year 647	7,764	−23.2
5% a year 531	6,372	−36.9
10% a year 294	3,528	−65.1
With-profits annuity		
Anticipating 3.5% growth 583	6,996	−30.8
Anticipating 7.64% growth 826	9,912	− 1.9
Index-linked 554	6,648	−34.2

The annuity payments reduce by half to the wife should the husband die first.

Source: Equitable Life

The implications of these annuity values to Andrew and any other person taking the benefits on a pension contract are considered shortly. But first we look at the annuity rates offered to one of Andrew's colleagues, Mavis Lawe, who is retiring at age 60. Being a widow, she is only concerned with annuities on her own life.

Mavis discovers that the annuity rates for women at her age are some 10 per cent lower than the corresponding rates for men and as such she will get a 10 per cent smaller pension from her savings compared with a man. Although Mavis considers this to be sex discrimination, particularly as her elder sister is retiring from a final salary company pension scheme and receiving the same pension as a man, life companies are permitted to quote different rates and terms for men and women, providing their calculations are based on firm actuarial data. The mortality rates used by actuaries to calculate annuity rates conform to this requirement.

Table 17

Pension annuity bought with £100,000 cash – Woman aged 60			
	Monthly	Year	Reduction in starting income
	£	£	%
Level annuity	783	9,396	—
Annuity increasing by			
3% a year	587	7,044	−25.0
5% a year	471	5,652	−39.8
10% a year	242	2,904	−69.1
With-profits annuity			
Anticipating 3.5% growth	523	6,276	−33.2
Anticipating 7.64% growth	767	9,204	− 2.0
Index-linked	494	5,928	−36.9

Source: Equitable Life

The Equal Opportunities Commission has been trying for several years to get the law changed so that both life and general insurance companies have the same rates for men and women on all contracts. But this book is concerned with the situation at present, and the lower annuity rates for women compared with men reflect their greater life expectancy. In simple terms, the life company, on average, pays the annuity for a longer period to women than to men.

In selecting the annuity, the purchaser has to consider for himself or herself:

- What do I need to live on now?
- How long am I going to live?
- What will be the level of inflation while I am alive?
- What will happen to my dependants when I die?

The overwhelming inclination of both Andrew and Mavis is to do what the majority of self-employed people have done when buying an annuity, and select the one with the highest starting value, that is, a level annuity on their own life, simply by considering only the first factor and stating that they cannot live on any lesser amount. If they consider the other factors at all, then their attitude is that they do not know how long they will live, what will happen to inflation, and that their spouses could die before they do.

Andrew is 65, so his life expectancy is 14.6 years, as explained in chapter one. But he is married, and his wife, Alison, is three years younger. Their combined life expectancy, that is the average time when the second person dies, is 23.3 years. Mavis at 60 has a life expectancy of 22.5 years.

Table 18. Decline in real value of a level annuity – Man aged 65.

	Inflation rate		
Age	3% £	5% £	7.5% £
65	952	952	952
66	924	907	886
67	897	863	824
68	871	822	766
69	846	783	713
70	821	746	663
71	797	710	617
72	774	677	574
73	752	644	534
74	730	614	497
75	708	584	462
76	688	557	430
77	668	530	400
78	648	505	372
79	629	481	346
80	611	458	322
81	593	436	299
82	576	415	278
83	559	396	259
84	543	377	241
85	527	359	224
86	512	342	208
87	497	325	194
88	482	310	180
89	468	295	168
90	455	281	156
91	441	268	145
92	429	255	135
93	416	243	126
94	404	231	117
95	392	220	109
96	381	210	101
97	370	200	94
98	359	190	88
99	348	181	81
100	338	173	76

Andrew should know what will happen to the real value of his pension over his just expected lifetime if he takes the level annuity just on his life.

Tables 18 and 19 show how inflation eats into the real value of the annuity. With inflation averaging 5 per cent a year, the value of the annuity is halved after 14.6 years, while with inflation running at 7.5 per cent, the annuity value is halved after 9.5 years.

Tables 20, 21 and 22 show how the annuities with guaranteed increases grow in value over the years, compared with the level annuity. Each of the three illustrated increasing annuities passes the level annuity after about 9–10 years – two-thirds of Andrew's life expectancy and less than half that of Mavis's life expectancy.

Andrew and Mavis cannot afford to take the risk of living too long without adequate financial protection, and since they are in good health they need to consider not just the first month's income, but the income in the succeeding months for many years into the future. They both need to compromise between the level of the starting income and future income increases.

Table 19. Decline in real value of level annuity

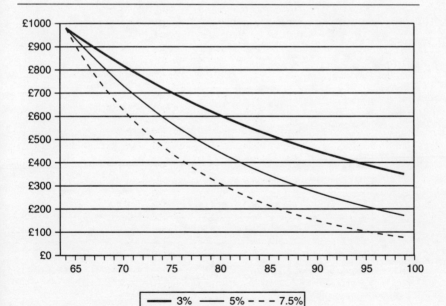

Table 20. Value of the monthly annuity over successive years – Man aged 65

	Level	Increasing at		
Year	£	3%p.a. £	5%p.a. £	10% p.a. £
1	952	758	640	390
2	952	781	672	429
3	952	804	706	472
4	952	828	741	519
5	952	853	778	571
6	952	879	817	628
7	952	905	858	691
8	952	932	901	760
9	952	960	946	836
10	952	989	993	920
11	952	1019	1042	1012
12	952	1049	1095	1113
13	952	1081	1149	1224
14	952	1113	1207	1346
15	952	1147	1267	1481
16	952	1181	1331	1629
17	952	1216	1397	1792
18	952	1253	1467	1971
19	952	1290	1540	2168
20	952	1329	1617	2385
21	952	1369	1698	2624
22	952	1410	1783	2886
23	952	1452	1872	3175
24	952	1496	1966	3492
25	952	1541	2064	3841

Table 21. Growth in annuity payments – Man aged 65

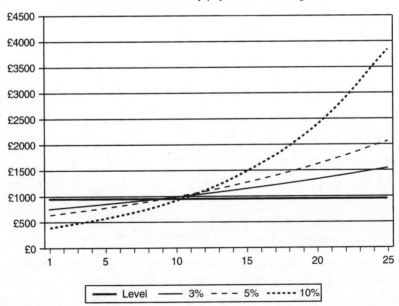

Table 22. Value of the monthly annuity over successive years – Woman aged 60

| | Level | Increasing at | | |
| | | 3%p.a. | 5%p.a. | 10%p.a. |
Year	£	£	£	£
1	783	587	471	242
2	783	605	495	266
3	783	623	519	293
4	783	641	545	322
5	783	661	573	354
6	783	680	601	390
7	783	701	631	429
8	783	722	663	472
9	783	744	696	519
10	783	766	731	571
11	783	789	767	628
12	783	813	806	690
13	783	837	846	759
14	783	862	888	835
15	783	888	933	919
16	783	915	979	1011
17	783	942	1028	1112
18	783	970	1080	1223
19	783	999	1134	1345
20	783	1029	1190	1480
21	783	1060	1250	1628
22	783	1092	1312	1791
23	783	1125	1378	1970
24	783	1158	1447	2167
25	783	1193	1519	2384

At this stage they have to take a view on the future trend in inflation rates, a subject on which high-powered economists have different views.

(a) If inflation rates in the future remain low then Andrew and Mavis need only take out an annuity with a low annual rate of increase, say 5 per cent, and the sacrifice in the starting income is not too great.

(b) On the other hand, if inflation rates in future are going to vary, as they have in the past two decades, between the very high and the very low, then Andrew and Mavis ought to take out either an annuity with a high rate of increase, say 10 per cent, or play completely safe and take out an index-linked annuity. In this case, they would have to make a considerable sacrifice in the starting income.

If they take option (a) and inflation rates soar, then Andrew and Mavis will find the real value of their annuity eroded by inflation, though not quite at the same rate as if they took out a level annuity. If they take option (b) and inflation rates in the UK stabilise at a low level, then Andrew and Mavis will have made an unnecessary sacrifice in their starting income which will not be made up by subsequent increases.

Fortunately there is another alternative – a unit-linked or with-profits annuity.

Annuities with level or increasing payments are without-profit annuities. Future payments are pre-determined and the underlying investments are fixed-interest investments. Unit-linked and with-profits annuities have their future payments linked to funds investing wholly or mainly in real assets, generally equities, and the value of these funds can be expected to rise with, or faster than, inflation.

Unit-Linked Annuities

With a unit-linked annuity, the cash is notionally invested in units of a selected fund. The value of the annuity payments is determined by the bid price of the units underlying the annuity on the date the instalment is paid. If the bid price has risen since the last instalment, then the annuity payments are correspondingly increased, and vice versa when the unit price falls.

Unit-linked annuities suffer from two major defects:

- The starting value is low.
- The payments can fall in money terms when the market is depressed.

Under some contracts, the purchaser has the option of increasing the starting value of the annuity by assuming a certain amount of the anticipated growth at outset, up to 10 per cent a year. Future increases in the annuity payments will be lower.

Table 23

Year	Annuity value £
1992–93	1,000
1993–94	1,237
1994–95	1,279
1995–96	1,248

Source: Equitable Life

Table 23 shows how an individual would have fared investing in a unit-linked annuity, linked to the managed fund, anticipating 8 per cent growth, taken out on 1 August 1992.

The problem of variable payments can be reduced by taking out a with-profits annuity.

With-profits Annuities

With-profits annuities work similarly to with-profit pension contracts. The with-profits annuities offered by Equitable Life operate on the following basis:

- First, there is an initial guaranteed annuity payment made.
- Secondly, these payments are increased by a guaranteed 3.5 per cent a year.
- Next, the guaranteed payments are further increased by the declared bonus. Once that increase has been made it is guaranteed for all future payments. The guaranteed increase and the bonus are added to the existing guaranteed payments and become the new guaranteed payments.
- A final bonus is added to the payments, but it is not guaranteed.

If Andrew or Mavis select a with-profits annuity in its basic form, the starting value is low but the increases are substantial. But in a similar manner to unit-linked annuities, they can opt to anticipate the guaranteed growth and part of the bonus, up to 4.5 per cent (making a total assumed growth of 8 per cent), and incorporate this into the annuity payments.

Table 24

Year	Annuity £
1990–91	1,000
1991–92	1,019
1992–93	1,033
1993–94	1,032
1994–95	1,058
1995–96	1,056

The effect for Andrew is seen in Table 15, and for Mavis in Table 16. But even with an anticipated growth of 5.5 per cent, Equitable

Life's bonus record to date has enabled most annuity payments to increase each year, as seen in Table 23 for an annuity purchased 1 April 1990.

So, despite the poor stockmarket conditions in 1994, the bonus rate was maintained so that the value of the annuity did not fall, though some increases were small.

Making the Decision

Now that Andrew and Mavis have reviewed the range of annuities available to them and have studied the implications of each, they are ready to start making their decisions as to which type of annuity, bearing in mind the following points:

- First, they should both do some housekeeping arithmetic as to the amount of monthly income they need to live comfortably, allowing for all possible expenses, including house repairs, the cost of running a car and holidays. This can be a tiresome chore, but unless it is done Andrew and Mavis could make the wrong decisions, which they would regret later on.
- Next, they should look at their other sources of income, including the basic State pension to which both will be entitled.
- The difference between the two figures indicates the starting income to be provided by the pension savings.
- They should take the amount of pension savings and see what type of annuity can be secured to provide the starting income. Married individuals should make some provision for a pension to their spouses in the event of them dying first.
- Some compromise is probably necessary.

Andrew's Decision

Andrew follows these steps to make his decision:

(1) Andrew and his wife consider that a monthly income of £2,000 a month gross (£24,000 a year) would be the minimum income sufficient for them to live comfortably.

(2) The basic State pension is £5,083 a year – equivalent to £423.58 a month, though the pension is paid weekly, and some

months they will receive five weeks' pension and others four weeks' pension. This income increases each year in line with rises in the Retail Price Index.

(3) Andrew has savings which bring in an income of around £140 a month – about half this income comes from equities, thereby providing some protection against inflation. His wife has very little income. So Andrew reckons on receiving around £530 a month from other sources, leaving a minimum of £1,500 a month as starting income from his pension savings.

(4) The total value of his pension savings is £300,000. Andrew takes the maximum cash sum of 27.6 per cent, say £82,800, which he gives to his wife, Alison.

(5) She invests the £82,800 in a high-income unit trust yielding around 3.0 per cent net of basic-rate tax. This provides an annual income of £2,484 – a monthly equivalent of £207. This income should, over the long term, keep pace with inflation.

(6) This makes a total monthly income of £770 to date, leaving Andrew to purchase an annuity with a starting value of £1,230 from the remaining £217,200 value from his pension contracts.

(7) Andrew decides that buying an annuity with a 50 per cent spouse's benefit will provide for Alison when he dies.

(8) From Table 16 we see that Andrew can meet this requirement by purchasing a with-profits annuity from a company anticipating the 3.5 per cent guaranteed growth – a starting value of around £1,266 a month. The annual bonus declarations will provide future growth in the annuity value.

Andrew and his wife's combined total monthly income at outset will be made up as follows:

	£
Basic State pension (married couple)	423
Other income	140
Wife's income from unit trust	207
Income from the annuity	1,266
Total	2,036

The starting income target is met, but how will Alison fare when Andrew dies? The position if Andrew died tomorrow, assuming all assets pass to Alison, would be:

	£
Basic State pension (single person)	265
Other income	140
Income from the unit trust	207
Income from the annuity	633
Total	1,245

Alison's income would be around 60 per cent of the combined income – regarded as an adequate proportion – and she has the capital invested in the unit trust from which she can buy an annuity if required. This arrangement meets the need to provide adequately for a spouse.

Finally, what about future increases in income?

- The basic State pension rises in line with the Retail Price Index.
- The income from the unit trust should at least match inflation over the long term.
- The bonus declarations will provide an increasing income, though whether these bonuses, without the guaranteed 3.5 per cent annual increase, will consistently match inflation will depend on the underlying investment performance.

Andrew's decision appears to provide a reasonable compromise between the conflicting objectives.

It is interesting to note that had he invested the £300,000 in a level annuity on his own life the monthly income from the annuity would have been around £2,856, which with the basic State pension and the other income would have brought the total starting income to around £3,500 a month – three-quarters more than what Andrew and his wife will receive.

Investors need to discipline themselves to think of the future and not just the present when buying the pension.

Annuity payments from the proceeds of a pension contract are treated, generally, as earned income. The exception is retirement annuities, which are still paid after deduction of basic rate tax at source. Any over or under payment of tax (for non or higher rate taxpayers) is a matter between the individual and their own tax inspector. Life companies are now required to deduct tax on a Schedule E PAYE system, even though Andrew has been taxed on Schedule D while working as a solicitor. It can be confusing if individuals cash-in their pension contracts at different times (see chapter nine) and have bought annuities with different life companies.

Mavis' Decision

(1) Mavis considers that she can live comfortably on £1,200 a month (£14,400 a year).

(2) Her basic State pension is £3180 a year (£265 a month). Her savings, mostly in building society accounts, bring her in a monthly income of currently around £57. So, allowing for her income from her savings not increasing, Mavis should go for a minimum starting income of £900 a month.

(3) The total value of her pension savings is £115,000.

(4) A glance at Table 17, which provides current annuity values for Mavis, shows that she has problems. Any annuity which increases in value leaves her with too low a starting income. The only viable alternatives are:

- Either a level annuity or a with-profits annuity anticipating the maximum allowable bonus, or
- Reducing her living standards, so that she can take an increasing annuity with a lower starting income.

If she can manage on £1,000 a month, that is, an annuity with a starting income of £700 a month, she could afford to take out either an annuity increasing by 3 per cent a year, or a with-profits annuity anticipating 5 per cent of the bonus.

How Mavis envies her sister with her company pension, but, not wishing to cut her standard of living just yet, Mavis opts for the with-profits annuity anticipating the full bonus and relying on the increases to her State pension, and a good bonus performance to provide her with her future pension increases.

Mavis's financial position can be mitigated a little if she takes the maximum cash sum and invests in an ordinary purchased life annuity.

Staggered Vesting

Andrew and Mavis have an alternative approach known as Staggered Vesting or Phased Annuities, whereby instead of cashing-in their contracts at retirement, they make partial cash-ins each year. This is explained in the next chapter.

Income Withdrawal

The 1995 Finance Act introduced the Income Withdrawal facility, which offers individuals flexibility in taking benefits from personal pension contracts.

Under this facility, individuals take their tax-free cash sum entitlement and then have a choice. They can either buy an annuity with the balance of the contract value or defer buying the annuity and draw income direct from the contract, through the life company, leaving the remaining fund invested and continuing to grow. The annuity can subsequently be bought at a time of the individual's choosing, providing it is bought, at the latest, on the individual's 75th birthday.

Details of the operation of the facility and the factors that should be taken into account in deciding whether or not to use the facility are described in chapter nine.

The facility does not apply to the old style Retirement Annuity Contracts. Persons with these contracts wishing to take their benefits direct from the contract must still buy an annuity with the balance of the contract value after taking the tax-free cash sum.

However, they can take income direct from the contract and defer buying an annuity by transferring from a Retirement Annuity Contract into a personal pension contract at the time when benefits are required. But it does mean that the amount of the tax-free cash sum is based on personal pension rules, that is a maximum of 25 per cent of the value, and not the usually more favourable Retirement Annuity Contract rules.

No charge is usually made if the transfer is arranged within the same company. Equitable Life does not charge its policy holders who transfer from a Retirement Annuity Contract to a personal pension.

Employee's Pension

Now we turn to an employee buying a pension, and we need to consider two separate company schemes – the defined benefit final salary schemes and the money purchase schemes.

Final Salary Schemes

As far as the employee is concerned, the pension at the normal pension age of the scheme is already determined – indeed it is the *raison d'être* of basing the scheme on an employee's earnings at or near retirement. As explained earlier, the pension also includes an automatic spouse's pension, and future pension increases are determined by the employer and trustees. The employee has no say and no decisions to take in this respect, although there are certain implications if the employee retires early or defers retirement, dealt with in the next chapter.

The only major decision an employee retiring at normal pension age must make is whether to commute part of his or her pension for a tax-free cash sum, and, if so, what to do with the cash.

Employees, on reaching retirement, will be given the following information:

- The full amount of pension.
- The maximum cash available and the consequent reduced pension.
- In each case it should also show the spouse's pension from the death of the employee. In many schemes, taking the cash sum does not affect the spouse's pension.

The employee can now see how much pension is given up in return for the cash.

Converting taxable pension into tax-free cash, at face value, usually looks like a good bargain. But there are one or two considerations to take into account before making the decision, considerations similar to those facing Andrew Foresite described earlier:

- Is the remaining pension sufficient to live on?
- If not, can the employee get a higher income by taking the cash and buying an annuity? He needs to remember that future pension increases from the company may be based on the lower pension.

Employees retiring from a public sector scheme automatically receive a cash sum and they only have to decide on how to invest that cash and whether their pension needs boosting by using the cash sum.

Employees receive their pension with full tax deducted under the PAYE system, as they did when receiving their salary or wages. The scheme receives a tax coding from the employee's tax office and makes the appropriate tax deduction. If employees are receiving pensions from more than one scheme, then they need to check that the combined tax charge is correct – there could be problems, especially if overall the employee is in a higher-rate tax bracket.

Additional Voluntary Contributions

Those employees who were prudent enough to pay additional pension contributions into an AVC scheme now have to decide what to do with the savings they have accumulated. Here there are different rules imposed by financial legislation, depending on when the employee took out the AVC arrangement.

If he or she took out the arrangement on or after 8 April 1987, then the accumulated value must be used to buy a pension, and the tax-free cash sum has to be obtained by commuting part of the main company pension. Some pension schemes buy the annuity for the employee on the same terms as the main pension is commuted, and it becomes part of the main pension qualifying for pension increases. But in most schemes and with free-standing AVCs the employee has to buy his own annuity. The considerations that should be taken into account in buying the annuity are similar to those stated above for buying an annuity with the commuted cash sum.

If the AVC was taken out before 8 April 1987, then the employee can take the accumulated value in cash, subject to Inland Revenue limits.

However, the total cash sum available at retirement from the AVC arrangement and from the company scheme is unchanged at the Inland Revenue limits – maximum of one-and-a-half-times final earnings. So the employee with such an AVC arrangement can use his or her savings towards the total cash sum and commute less pension from the main scheme, and therefore does not have to make any decisions regarding buying an annuity.

In the unlikely event of the AVC value exceeding the maximum cash sum, then the surplus must be used to buy a pension.

Advice

The company pensions department cannot advise the employee on any financial aspect of the employee's retirement, even if they wanted to, because of the requirements of the 1986 Financial Services Act, although the department may be able to recommend a financial adviser.

What the employee must not do is take the cash with no preconceived idea of how to use it and then just leave it in the bank.

Money Purchasing Schemes

Now the restrictions imposed by the Inland Revenue on benefits from company schemes really bite, particularly for director and executive schemes.

Those in company money purchase schemes usually have very little say in the form of benefits bought with the value of the savings accumulated for the employee. If the employee is retiring, then the pension has to be bought at the time of retirement. There is no flexibility, as with personal pensions, as to when to take the benefits.

The pensions are purchased by the trustees of the scheme in accordance with the rules of the scheme. These rules may be rigid in that they prescribe a certain type of annuity with certain increases and an automatic spouse's pension if the employee is married. The trustee is under no obligation to consult with the member over his or her choice or wishes; neither is the trustee obliged to seek the best annuity rate so that the employee receives the maximum pension for his money. Indeed, if the scheme's adviser is the representative of one life company then that adviser can only recommend that company's annuities – which is fine if the life company concerned offers competitive annuity rates, but far from satisfactory if it does not.

Where an employee is consulted by the trustees as to his or her wishes, then he or she faces similar problems to those people with personal pensions described earlier.

Controlling Directors and Executives

The situation is different for controlling directors and executives retiring from their company and taking the benefits, since they are also the trustees of the scheme and therefore can implement their own wishes.

Here we meet Cyril Wise-Mann, a controlling director of a family business. Cyril set up an executive pension arrangement when they became available in 1973. Having reached age 65, he now wishes to cease work and take the benefits from the scheme. The choices facing Cyril are essentially the same as if he were buying the pension from a personal pension contract, namely:

- When to cash-in his contracts.
- How much of the benefits to take as a tax-free cash sum.
- What type of annuity to buy with the remaining value.

But now the Inland Revenue imposes far more restrictions on the choices facing individuals in respect of all these three decisions compared with those on personal pensions, simply because it is a company scheme.

When to Cash-in

Technically, controlling directors have to take the benefits when they reach normal pension age. In practice they can take the benefits when they want, within reason, through early or late retirement. If they want to stop working but do not wish to take the benefits at that time, then they do this by remaining on the company board and drawing director's fees and remuneration.

Cyril, however, has been cutting down on his involvement with the company and feels that now is the time to make a complete break.

Cash Sum

The executive must first check on the maximum benefits available from the scheme. If, as in the case of Cyril, the scheme has been in force for many years and has been adequately funded, the benefits available are the Inland Revenue maximum limits.

The maximum cash sum a director can take depends on when he set up the arrangement.

- For members joining schemes before 1987, the individual can take the maximum cash sum of one-and-a-half times final earnings at retirement if he or she has completed 20 years' service with the company, without having to qualify for a full pension. There is a reduced scale for service of less than 20 years, but there is no ceiling on those earnings to determine the cash sum.
- For employees joining schemes between 1987 and 1989, full cash can only be taken after 20 years' service if the scheme also provides a full pension, otherwise the cash is scaled down. There is a ceiling on the earnings of £100,000 in determining the cash sum.

- For employees joining schemes from 1989, the maximum cash is two-and-a-quarter times the pension with all benefits subject to the Cap mentioned earlier.

Buying the Annuity

Cyril qualifies for the maximum pension and has two choices of how to provide for it:

- the scheme buys the pension now, or
- the scheme pays the pension for the first five years after Cyril has retired, and then buys the annuity.

Under the first option, the scheme has to find the cash to buy the annuity now. This may cause problems in converting assets to cash, particularly if property is involved.

Under the second option, there are three factors to consider:

- The scheme has flexibility in arranging the cashing-in of its assets so that it can provide the cash to pay the pension for five years and then put down a cash sum to buy the annuity.
- If the individual dies during the five-year period, the scheme is only required to pay out the balance of the pension for the remainder of the five years. It does not have to buy the annuity. The cash thus saved can remain in the scheme, thereby reducing the contributions of the other members remaining, if there are any, or be returned to the company, less a tax charge.
- However, the scheme is taking a risk on the movement in annuity values over the five-year period. If annuity rates move down over a period because interest rates have fallen, the eventual overall cost to the scheme is higher, while if interest rates move up the overall cost is lower.

Cyril is in good health and decides to buy the annuity now. He is earning £90,000 a year. So the maximum benefits are:

- either a pension of £60,000 a year, or
- a cash sum of £135,000 and reduced pension, the amount of which depends on the commutation factors agreed with the Inland Revenue.

The value of Cyril's executive pension arrangements is £1,000,000; now he runs into problems with the Inland Revenue limits.

Cyril's wife is three years younger than him. If he bought a level annuity with a 50 per cent spouse's pension with the £1,000,000, then from the rates shown in Table 16 the pension would be around £101,000 a year – well above the limits. Indeed, Cyril has so much cash accumulated in his executive pension plan that his problem is to buy an annuity which will use up all this cash. He can buy an annuity for himself and his wife with the maximum starting amount and a high rate of future increases. Referring again to Table 16 the following annuities will keep within the limits:

- 5 per cent increase – annuity around £63,700
- 10 per cent increase – annuity around £35,300
- Index-linked annuity – annuity almost £66,500

Cyril has to consider both the starting value of the annuity and the effect of inflation. But the Inland Revenue imposes certain restrictions on future pension increases that did not apply to annuities bought with personal pensions. Effectively, the annuity payments cannot exceed the value of the maximum permissible pension increased by the Retail Price Index since retirement. This rule has little practical effect on ordinary employees in retirement, because very few retire on the maximum pension. But it can impact director and executive pensions because many start with the maximum pension.

So if Cyril took out an annuity with a guaranteed 10 per cent increase, and if these increases meant that the annuity payments eventually overtook the initial maximum pension increased with the RPI, then the annuity increases would be restricted. So Cyril would not be any better off buying an annuity with a starting value below that of the index-linked annuity. As such, Cyril decides to take out an index-linked annuity where the increases will be in line with rises in the RPI and thus provide protection against inflation without causing problems if inflation is low.

Cyril naturally wishes to take the maximum tax-free cash of £135,000. With the balance of £865,000, he buys an index-linked annuity with a starting amount of £4,792 a month – just over £57,500 a year gross. Alternatively, an annuity increasing at 5 per cent a year provides an annuity of £4,593 a month, just over £55,100 a year. The commutation factors agreed with the Inland Revenue mean that these benefits are just within the limits.

However, the Inland Revenue's insistence on the use of commutation factors could result in a paradoxical situation, that if the executive uses the full value of his pension arrangements to buy a pension he is within limits, but if he takes the maximum cash, the pension bought with the remaining value would exceed the limits. It must be emphasized that such problems only arise when the executive pension arrangements are well funded. Executives with pension arrangements that are not so well funded have to take similar decisions to those taken by Andrew Foresite in deciding on the type of annuity to buy.

9

EARLY AND LATE RETIREMENT

The Inland Revenue has two different regimes for company pensions and personal pensions, and these regimes have different impacts on the benefits provided. Nowhere is this more apparent than in the situation of early and late retirement.

The position regarding State pension benefits, both basic and SERPS, was discussed in chapters two and three – namely the normal pension age is currently 65 for men and 60 for women, with no provision for taking the benefits at an earlier age, although the individual can defer taking benefits for up to five years.

The first part of this chapter will deal with the situation for personal pensions, which affects mainly the self-employed. The second part will then consider the situation for company pensions.

Self-employed

Here we meet Terence Foresite, Charlie Easy-Going's father-in-law.

Phased Retirement

Terry has been saving for his retirement since 1956, when pension plans for the self-employed first became available. Having reached age 67, Terry thinks it is time to take things a little easier, though he has no intention of completely ceasing to work. He has saved through a series of Retirement Annuity Contracts, and their flexibility will allow him to phase his retirement, as he can cash-in his contracts and take the benefits at any time between his 60th and 75th birthday, both dates inclusive. There is no requirement to stop work in order to take the benefits and there are no other restrictions on the cash-in.

The Inland Revenue will allow individuals in certain occupations, mainly professional sports, to take the benefits before age 60. For example, footballers can take their benefits from age 35 and cricketers from age 40. Individuals in poor health are also permitted to take the benefits early. Otherwise, those in good health can take their benefits from their 50th birthday by switching their RACs into personal pensions.

There are advantages for Terry in delaying cashing-in his contracts for as long as he can:

- He has longer to make contributions and build up the existing funds on his pension contracts.
- Annuity rates increase with age.
- He can take a higher proportion of the value as a tax-free cash sum; this factor only applies to RACs, not the new-style personal pensions, where the maximum proportion that can be taken in cash is fixed at 25 per cent.
- If he dies, the full increased value of the contract is paid, free of income tax, into his estate although it may be liable to Inheritance Tax. This can, however, be avoided by writing the policy in trust. The provider will be able to advise on this.

Provided Terry has arranged a series of RACs that can be treated as separate contracts, he can cash-in some of those contracts and still continue to pay contributions on the remainder.

By adopting this flexible retirement strategy, Terry has much more freedom in his choice of annuity. For example:

- At the present time, Terry will still be associated with the business, drawing a salary and sharing in the profits.
- So the starting level of the annuity is of less relevance compared with what it will be in a few years time when Terry has finished work completely.
- At such Terry can take out an annuity with a low starting value and high increases.

At present Terry decides to take a with-profits annuity allowing for the full bonus growth. He will cash-in enough contracts so that the starting value of the annuity replaces about three-quarters of the income reduction from the business. Since his expenses can be expected to be less, he does not need full income replacement, unless he becomes addicted to the golf club.

Terry intends to review his position every year and cut down his involvement in the business and replace a high percentage of the lost income by cashing-in more contracts. In later years, he can take out annuities with a higher starting income and lower increases if desired. It is very much a case of making decisions at the time in the light of prevailing circumstances, and clearly Terry has benefited from the flexibility of personal pensions by retiring late and phasing out his retirement over a lengthy period.

However, he should be aware that annuity rates could drop if interest rates fall during the period he is phasing out his retirement. If this happens, the increase in rates due to age would be offset by the effect of lower interest rates. With-profit annuities tend to be more stable in that the starting values are not directly dependent on current interest rate levels, as with ordinary annuities. Of course, if interest rates rise over the period, annuity rates will correspondingly rise, and Terry will have a third advantage from delaying taking the benefits.

Taking the Benefits Early

But had Terry wished to or been forced to retire earlier, say at age 60, then the factors described above would have worked against him – the value of the fund accumulated would have been much lower and annuity rates would also have been lower.

One of the features stressed by some salesmen promoting personal pensions is the ability to take the benefits from age 50; what tends to be omitted in the sales patter is that benefits at age 50 will be small in comparison with those at a later ages, simply because:

- The maximum contribution levels are low up to age 50 and the individual does not have the time to build up a sizeable fund.
- The annuity rates are so low at that age. The rate for level payments at age 50 for each £100,000 is £9,024 a year for men and £8,544 a year for women. This compares with an annuity of £11,424 at age 65 for men – 27 per cent higher, and an annuity of £9,396 at age 60 for women – 10 per cent higher.

It is difficult to see how an individual can use personal pensions to acquire adequate benefits at a comparatively early age.

Playing the Market

The actuary of the life company bases the calculation of his annuity rates on current fixed-interest yields on medium-term stocks, that is, stocks with a remaining period to redemption of around seven to ten years. When these yields change, the actuary revises his annuity rates accordingly – increasing the rates when the yields rise and lowering them when yields fall.

An individual retiring now could find himself in the position that his annuity payments are lower than they would have been had he taken them a few months earlier. It is often suggested that when interest rates are falling, as they did during 1990 and 1991, then individuals due to retire and take their benefits in a few months' time should take their benefits early before annuity rates fall.

Such advice is more relevant if the individual has been saving through with-profits contracts. Once the bonus is declared and vested, the cash-in value of the contract does not increase, or only increases marginally, until the next declaration.

However, the interest rates quoted by Government, banks and building societies relate to cash and deposit investments. While yields on longer-term fixed-interest stocks move with interest rate changes, the movement is not 100 per cent in line. Medium-term yields during 1990 remained remarkably stable, while short-term interest rates moved down steadily.

Tables 25 and 26 show the movement in annuity rates over the past five years for a man aged 65 for level payments with a purchase price of £10,000. They vary from a high of £1,393 in October 1991 to a low of £1,064 in January 1994 – a 24 per cent variation between the high and the low values.

It is easier to recommend that an individual delay taking benefits because the fund increases in value and annuity rates rise with age, which may mitigate against a fall in rates due to yield changes. It is much trickier to advise someone to take benefits earlier. For unless annuity rates do fall, the individual would have bought the pension from a lower fund at an earlier age. Care needs to be taken over recommending taking the benefits several months in advance, and any advice should be confined to cashing-in a few weeks early.

Anyone considering taking benefits early to get ahead of an anticipated annuity rate reduction should obtain a quotation from the life company. Life companies will usually hold an annuity quotation for several days, sometimes for about three weeks. By obtaining a quotation, the individual has a little time to see whether interest rates are moving and decide on a course of action.

Table 25. Amount of annuity bought with £10,000 – Man aged 65

Start date of annuity	Amount of annuity £ per annum
October 1, 1991	1,393
December 1, 1991	1,363
March 1, 1992	1,344
July 1, 1992	1,307
December 1, 1992	1,250
April 1, 1993	1,213
August 1, 1993	1,194
November 1, 1993	1,139
December 1, 1993	1,102
January 1, 1994	1,064
April 1, 1994	1,121
May 1, 1994	1,158
June 1, 1994	1,194
August 1, 1994	1,232
September 1, 1994	1,194
October 1, 1994	1,232
December 1, 1994	1,194
February 1, 1995	1,232
May 1, 1995	1,194
June 1, 1995	1,087
July 1, 1995	1,125
October 1, 1995	1,087
November 1, 1995	1,106
January 1, 1996	1,069
March 1, 1996	1,087
May 1, 1996	1,106

Source: Equitable Life

Table 26. Amount of annual annuity bought with £10,000 – Man aged 65

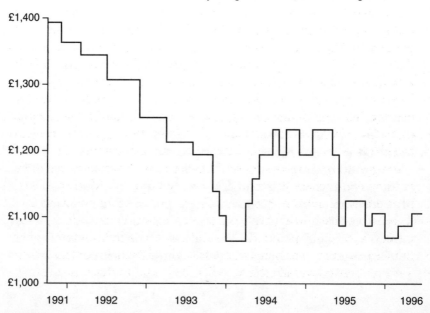

Switching

Those who have been investing their pension contracts in equities, property, managed funds, or even fixed-interest, should switch their investments systematically into cash or with-profits over the final year or two before cashing-in and taking the benefits.

When the equity market is rising, it is very tempting to ignore this advice and to stay in equities. If this gamble has paid off and the time for cashing-in the benefits is approaching, then the pension holder would be well advised not to take any further risks and switch immediately. With only a few weeks left, the only realistic option is to switch into a cash fund.

History has shown that the stockmarket can fall dramatically overnight, as it did in October 1987, and take a while to recover. Or it can move steadily down as it did in 1990 before recovering in 1991. Individuals should be wary of taking chances with their pension savings.

Staggered Vesting/Income Withdrawal

The flexibility over the timing of taking benefits and the facility for taking income from a personal pension contract and buying the annuity later, instead of buying the annuity immediately, were mentioned in chapter eight. Terence is interested in both these facilities, particularly as annuity rates still seem to be low, and wishes to know more on how both operate.

As stated earlier, individuals can take benefits under a personal pension at any time between their 50th and 75th birthdays, both dates inclusive. If contracts are not cashed-in until required, it provides a longer time for building up the fund. Also annuity rates increase with age when they are bought. So a combination of a greater fund and higher annuity rates means that if Terence delays cashing-in contracts for as long as possible, then he will receive a larger tax-free cash sum and higher annuity payments.

Staggered vesting is simply the process of cashing-in personal pension contracts in stages as benefits are required. Many personal pension policies are now written as a series of small contracts and Terence can cash-in as many or as few as he likes when he likes. If the process is carefully planned, the resulting benefits should be higher than if an annuity was bought at outset with the whole contract when Terence started to take the benefits. But expert advice is essential.

However, annuity rates vary much more with changes in interest rates, as seen earlier. Terence does not want to cash-in even a few contracts when annuity rates are low. This is where the withdrawal facility applies, whether some or all of the contracts are being cashed-in.

So the first step is to decide when to take the benefits. For many individuals the choice on timing is restricted to a few weeks after they cease working.

Next, the tax-free cash sum has to be taken at outset. The facility does not allow individuals to take income, but defer taking the cash sum until the annuity is bought. Once the cash sum has been taken, the individual then has the choice between:

- buying an annuity straightaway, or
- making withdrawals from the underlying funds and buying an annuity later.

The previous chapter described the process of buying an annuity. Now Terence has to consider how the income withdrawal operates.

- First, Terence has to decide on the amount of income which he wants to take from the contract over the next 12-month period, measured from the date benefits are taken, varies between a maximum and minimum limit. The maximum limit represents an hypothetical level annuity on the life of the individual, with the minimum limit being 35 per cent of the maximum.

The maximum limit is obtained from tables supplied by the Government Actuary based on the investor's age at the time the benefits are taken, the yield on the Financial Times-Actuaries 15 year gilt index (to the lower ¼ per cent) on the 15th of the month previous to the month in which the benefits are taken and the gross value of the underlying fund in the personal pension contract. There are different values for men and women, as with annuities.

Table 27 shows the income limits for individuals taking benefits in August 1996 – based on a yield of 8 per cent and an underlying fund value of £100,000.

- Second, Terence has to decide how to continue investing the remaining balance of the funds in the contract while

withdrawing income. This decision is crucial as will be
seen later.

- The withdrawal limits are fixed for three years. At the end
  of this period fresh limits are calculated based on the
  investor's age and gilt yields at the time and the value of
  the remaining fund.
- Finally, Terence has to decide when to stop taking income
  and buy the annuity with the remaining funds in his
  personal pension contract. He can do this at any time,
  but no later than his 75th birthday.

Putting the first and second points together, the investment
return that Terence must achieve on the balance of funds must
at least make up the income he has taken out. The greater the
annual amount withdrawn, the greater the investment return that
must be achieved on the balance of the funds.

As seen earlier in the book, the highest returns are obtained from
investment in equities. But this is also the most volatile of investments – there are years when returns on equities are negative. This
is not such a problem when building up funds, but can be disastrous
in the short term when taking income from the fund in a year when
equity returns are negative.

Investing in cash for safety is, paradoxically, courting disaster – the
general level of return is too low to make up the income withdrawn.

A combination of high withdrawals and/or poor investment
returns can deplete the fund rapidly so that when the annuity is
eventually bought, the resulting annuity is lower than that which
would have been bought at outset.

To show what could happen, Terence obtained illustrations
produced in accordance with PIA rules, based on three investment
returns. These are shown and described in Table 28.

This shows first the importance of the investment return
achieved on the balance of the funds and secondly the need to
keep withdrawals as low as possible.

The table shows that to obtain a steady income from the fund
assuming investment returns of 9 per cent a year, the amount of
income withdrawn each year – £10,300 – is less than provided from
buying an annuity – £11,627 a year. Investment returns have to
average around 12 per cent a year in order to make withdrawals at a
high level without seriously depleting the fund. An investment
return of only 6 per cent a year is disastrous.

- However, what interests Terence most about income withdrawal is the benefits available to his family should he die before buying an annuity.

In this case, his wife or dependants have the choice of:

(a)   continuing making withdrawals as if he were still alive,
(b)   buying an annuity straightaway,
(c)   taking the cash value of the fund in the contract, less a 35 per cent tax charge, and having it paid into Terence's estate.

This latter feature means that the remaining fund in the personal pension can be passed on to Terence's children, in contrast to buying an annuity, where if he dies after any guaranteed period, there is no money to pass on to the next generation.

So the general advice to Terence, if he wants to take income from the personal pension contract, is:

- Keep the amount withdrawn in each 12-month period as low as possible, preferably the minimum.
- Invest the remaining funds in either a with-profits fund or a guaranteed fund – the best compromise between high returns and low volatility.
- Do not make the decision solely on the death benefit. Terence could live to 75 and have to buy an annuity.
- Look at the position at least once a year at the end of each 12-month period and be prepared to change strategy immediately, if necessary. Professional advice is paramount at all stages. The PIA requires every individual to receive a statement of the situation in the personal pension contract once a year.

The potential dangers with income withdrawal should not be overlooked, ignored or minimised. Terence and every other individual contemplating income withdrawal should fully understand these dangers and be prepared to accept the risks.

In particular, if the vast majority of an individual's income in retirement will come from the personal pension, then as a general rule, the individual should buy an annuity at outset.

Income withdrawal is possibly best used in conjunction with staggered vesting – cashing-in a few contracts at a time. But such a combination will need careful planning and monitoring.

Table 27. Annual Income Withdrawal Limits for August 1996
    – Fund value £100,000 (yield 8 per cent)

| Age | Men | | Women | |
| | Maximum | Minimum | Maximum | Minimum |
£	£	£	£	
55	9,500	3,325	8,900	3,115
56	9,700	3,395	9,000	3,150
57	9,800	3,430	9,100	3,185
58	10,000	3,500	9,200	3,220
59	10,100	3,535	9,400	3,290
60	10,300	3,605	9,500	3,325
61	10,500	3,675	9,600	3,360
62	10,700	3,745	9,800	3,430
63	10,900	3,815	10,000	3,500
64	11,200	3,920	10,100	3,535
65	11,400	3,990	10,300	3,605
66	11,700	4,095	10,500	3,675
67	11,900	4,165	10,800	3,780
68	12,300	4,305	11,000	3,850
69	12,600	4,410	11,300	3,955
70	12,900	4,515	11,600	4,060

Table 28. Income Withdrawal Illustration – Man aged 67 taking benefits
    in August 1996 – Fund value, after tax-free cash taken, is £100,000.

Option A – buying a level annuity on his life – £11,627 a year
Option B – taking income withdrawals from the contract.
Maximum/Minimum withdrawal £11,900/£4,165 a year

(i) If withdrawals of £10,300 a year are made until age 75, and the investment
return on the balance of the fund is 9 per cent a year, then the value of the fund
remaining at age 75 would be £74,800 and this would be sufficient to buy an
annuity of £10,300 a year assuming interest rates at the time were 7.5 per cent.
(ii) If the same level of withdrawals were made, that is £10,300, for three years, but
the investment return was only 6 per cent a year, the withdrawal in the fourth
year would have to be reduced to £9,470 a year for another three years and in
the seventh year to £8,660. The remaining fund at 75 would be £59,000 and the
annuity secured, assuming an interest rate of 5 per cent, would be £7,200 a
year.
(iii) However, if withdrawals of £10,300 a year were made for the first three years
and the investment return was 12 per cent a year, the withdrawal in the fourth
year would be increased to £11,200 for the next three years and to £12,300 in the
seventh year. The remaining fund at 75 would be £94,200 and this would secure
an annuity of £14,500 a year, assuming an interest rate of 10 per cent.
Basis laid down by the Personal Investment Authority.

Employees

The problem facing many employees over the past decade has been
early retirement through redundancy rather than late retirement,
though that situation could change over the next decade as the
numbers of young people coming into the labour market diminish.

Personal Pensions

Employees saving for their retirement through personal pensions who take early or late retirement are in a similar situation to the self-employed.

They do not have to cash-in their benefits simply because they have stopped work, though they cannot make any further contributions unless they resume work. On the other hand they probably need to take an income within months of stopping work. The flexibility in cash-in means that they can defer taking an annuity until they have used up any Social Security benefits and any cash payments from the company. As already stated, there are no facilities for early payment of the State pensions.

Cash payments from the company are more likely to be given to executives, senior managers and other employees taking early retirement as part of a redundancy exercise than if the early retirement is purely voluntary on the part of the employee. Here, the employee buying a pension at an early age faces the problem of an inadequate fund buying annuities at low rates. It is doubtful whether an employee in this situation would receive any financial help from the employer other than the cash sum payment, and even if the employer was willing to enhance the employee's pension, it is difficult to see how this could be done on a tax-efficient basis.

Employees need to consider very carefully how best to invest any cash available to boost their income. It will involve following steps very similar to those described in the previous chapter on buying the pension and investing the cash sum.

Those considering early retirement on a voluntary basis should check on the benefits before announcing their intentions to anyone else; this is because the odds are that the pension will be too low to make such action feasible. An employee taking voluntary early retirement is likely to need at least part-time work for some years until the personal pension contract provides an adequate pension.

Company Money Purchase Schemes

The situation could be different for employees in company money purchase schemes who retire early, as compared with employees having personal pensions, in that the employer is in a position to enhance the pension. Otherwise these employees face similar problems to those described above with personal pensions.

Late retirement poses few problems. The accumulated fund continues to grow and buys a pension at a higher annuity rate. Problems can arise with the Inland Revenue limits if the underlying investment performance is good and/or the employee continues to pay contributions.

Final Salary Schemes – Early Retirement

As mentioned in chapter three, the employer is in a position to set his own level of early retirement benefits since, unlike individuals, the employer is not controlled by the marketplace. If the employer wants to pay generous early retirement benefits within Inland Revenue limits, then all he or she has to do is pay the required higher costs.

The early retirement penalty on actuarial grounds is effectively of the same magnitude as the penalty shown above when retiring early on a personal pension. But many schemes mitigate the penalty for employees retiring a few years before normal pension age, and some may even eliminate the penalty close to retirement. For example, a scheme with a normal retirement age of 65 could impose no penalty for retirement at ages 63 and 64, and for retirement at ages 60, 61 and 62 a penalty of 1 per cent for each year retirement is taken early.

In addition, many schemes pay a 'bridging pension' to men retiring between ages 60 and 65 until the basic State pension becomes payable at age 65. But if employees want to retire several years early, say at 55, then a more normal penalty tends to be imposed, with no bridging pension.

Employers have to take care that when an employee retires early the pension at 65 for men or 60 for women is at least equal to the Guaranteed Minimum Pension (GMP). Sometimes the pension paid early has not been increased sufficiently by the time the employee reaches State pension age and the scheme has to give the pension a boost to bring it up to the GMP level.

Employees interested in retiring early should obtain a quotation of the benefits available from the scheme before they start making arrangements, as they need to know what pension they would receive in order to plan their early retirement.

Additional Voluntary Contributions

One factor used to promote AVCs is to tell employees they can be used to facilitate early retirement. And so they can – providing the employee starts paying contributions early in his working life and makes sufficiently high contributions.

But often, employees only think a few years ahead of the event that they would like to retire early, and the problems encountered are the same as those for early retirement with personal pensions. An AVC arrangement that will provide adequate benefits for a man at age 65 will fall short of requirements at age 60 and be pitifully inadequate at age 55.

Final Salary Schemes – Late Retirement

Late retirement benefits cause relatively few problems for employees who work beyond the normal pension age of the scheme.

Pension

There are two alternative practices regarding calculating the pension when an employee defers retirement:

- The employee continues to accrue years of service up to the Inland Revenue limits and usually continues to pay contributions. The pension when the employee ultimately retires is based on the usual formula of years of service and earnings at retirement. This method is favourable if the employee concerned has not completed his quota of accrued years at normal retirement. But there are two possible drawbacks:
  - (a)   An employee close to maximum pension at retirement can have problems with Inland Revenue limits.
  - (b)   If the terms on which the employee continues working involved a reduction in overall earnings, then the ultimate pension could be lower. The Inland Revenue allow the pension to be calculated on the average of the best three years' earnings out of the ten years prior to retirement. So any employee working after normal retirement, but on lower earnings, should check on the effects on the ultimate pension.

- The other method of ascertaining the pension when an employee defers retirement is to calculate the employee's pension at normal pension age and increase this pension by a given percentage for each month, say 1 per cent per month. This is known as pension enhancement.

Death-in-service

If the employee, having continued working after normal pension age, then dies before ultimately retiring, the death benefits can be:

- either the usual cash sum plus spouse's pension, or
- it is assumed that the employee retired on the day before he died. The benefits then paid are the guaranteed five years' pension payments in a cash sum, plus spouse's pension.

Retire and Re-hire

A practice adopted by some companies where the employee wishes to continue working and the employer wishes to retain his services in some capacity is to retire the employee at the normal pension age and re-hire him on contract for a fee. The employee becomes self-employed and therefore eligible to take out a personal pension. However, the Inland Revenue are now looking closely at this practice for employees. In addition, there is now legislation to prevent controlling directors from having personal pensions in these circumstances.

10

CHANGING JOBS

Employees are becoming far more mobile in their work and it is becoming increasingly rare for an individual to stay in one job for the whole of his or her working life.

Changing jobs can have a considerable impact on the ultimate pension, the impact depending very much on the type of pension arrangement.

Money Purchase Schemes

By their very nature, money purchase schemes are fully portable. The employee, on changing jobs, simply takes the pension contract to the new employer.

For example, Susan Briteyes from chapter six has contracted-out of SERPS with an appropriate personal pension, and has taken out a personal pension on top. If and when she leaves her present job with Forward Enterprises, she will take her personal pension contracts with her, and her new employer will handle the arrangements to continue to contract-out of SERPS and Susan will continue paying contributions into her personal pension. She may even persuade her new employer to contribute to her personal pension, even though the employer is not obliged to do this.

However, if employees are made redundant or leave an employer and cannot find another job, they cannot continue paying contributions into their personal pension contracts. Contributions can only be made from relevant earnings – earnings from employment or from being self-employed. The Inland Revenue does not accept investment income as relevant earnings.

It becomes slightly more complicated if the employee is in a money purchase company scheme. If the scheme is written as a group personal pension, the employee has his own personal pension contract which he takes to the next job.

But in most money purchase schemes, the employee has to cease contributions and leave his accumulated fund in the scheme to continue to grow until normal pension age. While it is possible to transfer the fund to a new employer's scheme, this does not seem to happen in practice. While the employee does not lose the value by leaving the fund in his old employer's scheme, he could face at retirement different bits of pension from different schemes, which is administratively messy for tax purposes.

Final Salary Schemes

These schemes particularly cause problems when an employee changes jobs, and much has been written on the plight of the 'early leaver' and the loss of pension benefits on changing jobs, compared with the benefits received by the employee who stays with the employer.

Over the past few years, the Government has brought in legislative requirements that have steadily improved the benefits available from final salary schemes to members who change jobs; unfortunately the situation is now more complex for employees.

Let us consider the position of two employees in Forward Enterprises.

Short-term Employees

Paula Purple, Peter Hard-Worker's secretary, is leaving Forward Enterprises. Since she has been with the company less than two years, she is entitled under the scheme rules to get her contribution refunded in cash, less a tax charge of 20 per cent.

Paula considers that this tax deduction is a 'rip off' by the company and the Inland Revenue, until the pensions department points out that she received 25 per cent tax relief on the contributions that she paid and that far from 'ripping her off' the Inland Revenue has treated her very well, and in fact her contribution payments have turned out to be a very favourable short-term investment – far better than had she put the money in a building society.

This refund of contributions represents the only occasion when an individual can get cash out of the pension scheme before retirement.

Longer-term Employees

Peter's assistant, John Grumbler, aged 35, is not treated so well.

He is leaving Forward Enterprises after ten years and would like to get his contributions refunded, even with a tax charge. But schemes are not permitted to make refunds to employees who have at least two years' service.

Instead, he has four choices as to how to deal with his accrued benefits in the pension scheme, FE Pensions. They are:

- leave the benefits in the scheme as a deferred pension, or
- take the cash equivalent of those benefits, known as a transfer value, and either:
  - (1) transfer the cash to his new employer's scheme, if there is one, or
  - (2) invest the cash in a Section 32 buy-out contract from a life company, or
  - (3) invest the cash in a protected rights personal pension.

DEFERRED PENSION

John is earning £24,000 at present. His deferred pension is calculated on the brick principle inherent in final salary schemes, based on his current pensionable earnings and length of service to the time of leaving the company.

As we saw in chapter six, FE Pensions, in accruing the benefits at 1/60th for each year of service, makes an allowance for the basic State pension. So John's current pensionable earnings are £24,000 less £4,770, that is £19,230; his deferred pension will be 10/60ths of £19,230: that is £3,205 payable from age 65.

This deferred pension has, under social security legislation, to be revalued each year. But it is split into two parts and each is revalued on a different basis.

- The first part is the Guaranteed Minimum Pension, invariably referred to as the GMP. The GMP is the equivalent benefit to that provided by SERPS and has to be increased by either:
  - (a) the rise in National Average Earnings or, if schemes are not prepared to accept this open-ended liability, they can

(b) revalue in line with National Average Earnings, but with a maximum of 5 per cent a year and pay a cash sum to the National Insurance fund, or

(c) revalue at a fixed rate of 7.5 per cent a year.

Most company schemes, including FE Pensions, revalue GMPs at 7.5 per cent a year.

- The remaining part of the pension has to be revalued in line with increases in the Retail Price Index up to a maximum of 5 per cent until the pension is taken. Pension schemes can give higher annual increases up to the full rise in the RPI. Public sector schemes, such as in the civil service, increase the GMP by National Average Earnings and the remaining pension by the rise in the RPI. But FE Pensions only increases deferred pensions above the GMP by the legal minimum.

John's deferred pension is split as follows:

	£
GMP	1,037
non-GMP	2,168
Total	3,205

Assuming inflation averages 5 per cent or more a year for the next 30 years, when he will be 65, John will receive a pension from FE Pensions of around £17,817 a year from age 65, consisting of:

	£
GMP	8,447
non-GMP	9,370
Total	17,817

This pension, once it becomes payable, will receive the statutory increases in the GMP element and the normal increases in the non-GMP element as for any other pension paid by the scheme.

This increase in deferred pensions looks reasonable. But over the past decades the growth in employees' earnings has on average outpaced the rise in inflation by 2.5 per cent a year. So if John had stayed with Forward Enterprises, and his earnings had risen by 7.5

per cent a year, he could have expected these first ten years' earnings to have produced a pension at age 65 of around £29,000 – half as much again as his deferred pension.

Had he been in a company money purchase scheme, the benefits from the first ten years' contributions would have been the same, whether he left or stayed with the company.

Despite all the improvements over the past decade, employees who stay with a company still get a better deal out of the company final salary pension scheme than those who leave the company, though the differential has been narrowed considerably.

TRANSFER VALUES

However, John does not have to leave his accrued pension benefits with FE Pensions. He has the legal right to an equivalent value of those benefits and can transfer them into another pension arrangement. He does not have to exercise that right immediately on leaving his employer, and can leave the accrued pension benefits with FE Pensions and transfer later. Indeed, he can exercise the right at any time up to one year before normal pension age, that is until he is 64.

John asks the pensions department of Forward Enterprises for a transfer value quotation while he is still with the company. Employees can ask for a transfer value quotation at any time, whether or not they have indicated their intention to leave the company; such requests should be kept confidential by the pensions department.

The transfer value is the present cash value of the deferred pension, with the amount of the pension payments made from the retirement of the employee discounted back to the time of the calculation. Social security legislation states that the transfer value must be equivalent to the deferred pension, although the method of calculation and the assumptions used are left to the professional judgement of the scheme's actuary, acting within guidelines laid down by the actuarial profession.

In John's case, the actuary to FE Pensions has to assume the following:

- The starting amount of the pension when John reaches 65.
- The rate at which John's pension will increase once it becomes payable. The actuary is required to consult with

the trustees over their practice in making pension increases, although it is impossible to say with certitude
what the position will be in 30 years' time. There is a
requirement for company schemes to increase pensions
by the rise in the Retail Price Index up to a maximum of 5
per cent a year. The actuary makes his assumption as to
how John's pension will increase after considering these
two factors.
- The rate of interest at which these payments are discounted back to the date of the calculation. The actuary
must take into account the current yield on gilts of the
appropriate term in determining the rate of interest to use
in discounting.

The assumptions used are crucial in determining the amount of
transfer value which John or any other employee changing jobs can
take to another pension arrangement. The actuary has to supply
the trustees with details of the assumptions used.

The calculations made by the actuary to FE Pensions produces a
transfer value of £18,653. John thinks this is a reasonable value,
though he would still like the cash in his pocket.

However, the flexibility allowed to actuaries within the professional guidelines to use their professional judgement in determining
the various factors can cause problems. It is quite common for two
employees in two different pension schemes providing identical
benefits to have the same deferred pension payable from the same
date, but have quite different transfer values because the actuary to
each scheme has made different assumptions. It is possible for the
transfer values quoted for the same deferred pension to vary by as
much as 25 per cent.

The actuary to FE Pensions appears to have adopted a basis
that is on the generous side. But with inflation rates and interest
rates coming down, the actuary could change his assumptions.
John needs to make sure that the actuary has either given a date
or stated the terms on which his transfer value figure remains
valid.

If John thinks that, with interest rates coming down, transfer
values can be expected to increase, then he does not have to take
the transfer value on leaving Forward Enterprises. He can leave
his deferred pension in FE Pensions and take a higher transfer
value later.

But John does not want to play the market, and just wants to transfer his benefits to another pension arrangement. His choices are:

- transfer to his new employer's scheme, or
- invest in a protected rights personal pension, or
- invest in a Section 32 buy-out.

TRANSFER TO A NEW COMPANY SCHEME

John Grumbler's new employer, Progressive Initiatives, has a company pension scheme – PI Pensions. Although company schemes have to give a leaving employee a transfer value out of the scheme, the scheme is not obliged to accept a transfer value into the scheme. PI Pensions will accept John's transfer value though, and quotes him the benefits secured by the value as a number of year's service.

John gets something of a shock when he receives the quotation. PI Pensions provides benefits very similar to FE Pensions. John, at the start, is receiving the same salary – £24,000 – as he was earning with Forward Enterprises. The pension benefits secured by 10 years' service with FE Pensions buys eight years and six months' service with PI Pensions. This means that his pension from PI Pensions at 65 after 30 years' service will be 38.5/60ths of £24,000 (£15,400) compared with the 40/60ths of £24,000 (£16,000) that he would have received from FE Pensions.

John is completely puzzled. The calculation of the benefits secured by a transfer payment into a scheme looks to be the reverse of the calculation to ascertain the transfer value out. And, by coincidence, the actuary to PI Pensions is also the actuary to FE Pensions and he is required, under the professional guidance, to use consistent assumptions for the calculation of the transfers in and for the transfers out.

The reason for the disparities in this case is that the calculation of the transfer-in value is not an exact replica backwards of the transfer-out calculation.

The actuary calculates what pension is secured at 65 by John's transfer value. This is then expressed as a percentage of John's anticipated earnings at 65. This percentage of 60 provides the number of added years. The actuary, in calculating the benefits secured by the transfer payment in, assumes that John's earnings at

Progressive Initiatives will increase in full, with no cut-off value of 5 per cent as was assumed for the transfer value out. As such, the pension at 65 secured a lower percentage of John's final earnings than the 10/60ths he had in his old scheme.

If John was starting with a salary of £30,000 at Progressive Initiatives then, because of the 5 per cent cut-off, the pension secured by the transfer in payment would be unchanged, but John's anticipated earnings at 65 would now be 25 per cent higher than if he started at £24,000, and so the proportion of the pension in terms of those final earnings would be lower, resulting in a lower number of added years – in this case six years and nine months.

Essentially, the transfer value provides the same pension in money terms, but the proportion this represents depends on the anticipated earnings at retirement.

This is a very simple example. If PI Pensions offered better benefits than FE Pensions then the number of added years secured by the transfer payment would be lower still, and vice versa.

If John's earnings at Progressive Initiatives rise faster than assumed by the actuary in his calculation, then John may do better by transferring his pension to the new scheme. But if his earnings fail to keep pace with the assumptions, then he may do better to consider the other alternatives.

However, John can invest his transfer value in a pension contract with a life company; this is the route taken by the majority of early leavers. He has the choice of investing in a protected rights personal pension or a Section 32 buy-out. The main difference between these two alternatives lies in the treatment of the GMP element of the transfer value.

PROTECTED RIGHTS PERSONAL PENSIONS

This contract operates on a purely money purchase basis, just like an ordinary personal pension, although the contract consists of two quite separate parts which have to be maintained throughout. The transfer value invested in the contract consists of two elements:

- the protected rights element, the cash value of the GMP, and
- the excess.

The protected rights element is invested in the first part of the contract and operates in a similar manner to an appropriate personal pension used to contract-out of SERPS. Benefits cannot be taken before State pension age unless the individual dies, and the accumulated value at State pension age has to be used to buy a pension on the same basis as an appropriate personal pension.

The excess part operates as an ordinary personal pension, including taking part of the value as a tax-free cash sum.

The contract has the same underlying investment funds for both parts.

SECTION 32 BUY-OUT

This is a hybrid contract of part defined benefits and part money purchase. Again, the contract is divided.

In the first part, the life company has to guarantee to pay the GMP entitlement in the deferred pension from State pension age – a benefit commitment. The life company calculates what proportion of the transfer value is required to invest to meet the GMP commitment. As such, the underlying investment tends to be restricted to with-profits. Many unit-linked life companies do not offer Section 32 buy-out contracts.

The second part operates as a money purchase contract, with the balance of the transfer value invested, with the accumulated value used to provide a tax-free cash sum and buy an annuity.

The operation of the two contracts and the differences are summarised in Table 29.

Which contract is the better for John? How does he make his choice?

A Section 32 buy-out tends to provide higher tax-free cash sums for controlling directors and highly-paid executives. Indeed many of these highly-paid employees for technical reasons find the benefits restricted under a protected rights contract compared with a buy-out. Such employees should take expert advice before making their decision.

But this does not apply to John, so how does he make his choice, particularly as the official benefit illustrations are of no help in comparing contracts.

John can only make his choice by understanding the benefit structure – does he want a pension guarantee as with the buy-out? – and investment risk – does he want complete freedom as with a protected rights? On balance, the vast majority of employees changing jobs invest their transfer payments in a protected rights personal pension, and John will probably do the same.

Table 29

Protected Rights Personal Pension	Section 32 Buy-out
(A) *Protected Rights* • The accumulated fund has to be used to buy a pension at State pension age on a unisex, unistatus basis, with the pension increasing at 3 per cent a year. • On early death the accumulated value must be used to buy a spouse's pension. If employee is single, value paid as a lump sum into the estate. • Complete investment freedom.	(A) *GMP Element* • GMP paid from the normal retirement date of the old company scheme. The pension can be paid earlier if the total pension on the whole contract at least equals the GMP. • Spouse's pension available should the individual die early. • Investment restricted.
(B) *Excess* • The benefits can be cashed-in wholly or partially at any time between the 50th and 75th birthdays. Up to 25 per cent of the combined value of the contracts can be taken as tax-free cash, providing it can be paid from the excess. The remaining value has to be used to buy an annuity, with complete freedom as to choice of annuity. • On early death, if the employee is married, up to 25 per cent of the combined value can be taken as tax-free cash, providing it can be paid from the Excess value. The remaining value used to buy an annuity for the spouse. • If the employee is not married the value can be taken in cash free of inheritance tax if written under trust for named beneficiary(ies) • Thus there is a complete difference of treatment on early death between couples who are married and those who are cohabiting • Complete investment freedom	(B) *Non-GMP Element* • Tax-free cash sum available on retirement depending on number of years' service and salary at time of transfer, taking limited RPI increases into account. • Remaining value at retirement used to buy an annuity, with complete freedom as to choice of annuity. • On early death, the fund value is paid in cash free of tax if written under trust. • Benefits subject to Inland Revenue limits. • Complete investment freedom.

John gets an official illustration of the benefits secured by his transfer value of £24,592 for a protected rights personal pension. He receives two illustrations, one for the protected rights and the other for the excess.

PROTECTED RIGHTS

The protected rights element of his transfer value amounted to £9,435. The illustration gave him two values:

- If the underlying investment showed a return of 0.5 per cent above National Average Earnings, the fund would be £9,357 at age 65 and this would secure a monthly pension of £46 (£552 a year). The pension would increase by 3 per cent a year and provide a 50 per cent widow's pension.
- If the underlying investment showed a return of 2.5 per cent above average earnings the fund would be £17,127 and this would secure a monthly pension of £132 (£1,584 a year).

Not surprisingly, John is completely confused. The values given assumed a real rate of return and expressed the fund value and pension at age 65 in today's terms, not the actual money values at 65.

But once he had grasped the meaning, he was in a position to compare with the current GMP element in his deferred pension of £1,037 a year. If the investment return in the protected rights portion of the personal pension earns only 0.5 per cent above earnings growth, John will do worse in the personal pension, with only £552 a year. But if the fund earns 2.5 per cent more than the average earnings growth, he will do better at £1,584.

If we go back to Table 9 in chapter four, we will see that life company-managed funds have on average achieved nearly 8 per cent above average earnings growth over the past ten years.

Now John looks at the illustration for the benefits secured by the non-GMP element in the transfer value of £15,157. This showed two figures:

- If the investments earned on average 6.0 per cent a year, then the fund value at age 65 would be £74,200, and the monthly annuity secured by this value would be £578 – £6,936 a year.
- If the investments earned 12 per cent a year, the fund value would be £387,000, securing a monthly annuity of £4,180 – £50,160 a year.

The illustration quoted amounts in money values at the time John reaches age 65, not in current values. So he cannot add the two parts of the pension together to get an overall pension which he can compare with his deferred pension. John has to discount these pension figures back 30 years to get a comparable figure, and the notes to the illustration contain discounting factors at interest rates of

4 per cent, 7 per cent and 10 per cent. Or he can project the deferred pension forward and compare with the above pension figures.

John's projected non-GMP deferred pension at age 65 was £9,655 a year – higher than the £6,936 annual pension illustrated on 6 per cent return, but well below the £50,160 annual pension at 12 per cent return.

But John has fallen into the trap of not comparing like with like. The annuity in the illustration is a level annuity, just on his life. The non-GMP part of the deferred pension will get increases and have a 50 per cent spouse's pension. We can assume that the increases will average 5 per cent.

If we look at Table 16 in chapter eight and compare a single life annuity with a joint annuity increasing at 5 per cent, the joint life starting annuity is almost 56 per cent of the level annuity.

So, in the above illustrations, we need to reduce the annuities values shown by 45 per cent to (i) £3,815 a year at 6.0 per cent investment return and (ii) £27,588 a year at 12 per cent investment return. If John had taken an index-linked annuity for comparison, these values would have been about a further 10 per cent lower.

John estimates that if the overall investment return achieved by the life company exceeds 8 per cent a year, then he will do better transferring from his deferred pension into a protected rights personal pension. He decides to make the transfer, while fully understanding the risk he is taking that the ultimate pension could be lower if the life company cannot produce this required investment return.

11

SOURCES OF ADVICE AND CONSUMER PROTECTION

It should now be obvious to all the characters in this book, and to anyone else really serious about saving for their retirement, that they need advice from experts. Where do they get that advice? What sort of advice will it be?

We saw in chapter five how Charlie Easy-Going planned his pension; this is how he reached the decision with his adviser.

The first thing Charlie, or any other individual, has to do is to choose the adviser:

- Charlie can seek advice from any one of the people he deals with in his business – his accountant, his solicitor, his bank manager or his insurance adviser, or
- he can go to the building society with which he has his savings, or
- he can go to firms with which he has had no previous dealings – a life company representative, an independent financial adviser or even a firm of consulting actuaries.

The main problem is choosing the *right* adviser.

In order to ensure an adequate income at retirement, Charlie needs to put aside substantial sums for a long period and then invest the accumulated savings to ensure that there is that adequate income. So what is Charlie looking for in an adviser?

Adviser Requirements

- The UK pensions market is extremely complex, so the adviser must have the necessary knowledge and expertise to give the best advice.

- There are large sums involved, and the investor is going to accept whatever recommendations are put before him or her, so the integrity of the adviser must be of the highest order.
- Individuals are going to be saving over many years, and will need to continually review and revise their arrangements, and therefore they need continuity from their adviser.

Charlie found that setting up a pension contract was far more complex compared with the simple matter of opening a deposit account with a building society. Charlie and the partnership have been dealing with the same firm of accountants for many years and are completely satisfied with the service provided. So he consulted his accountant. However, his accountant, being a small partnership, no longer gave in-depth investment advice to clients, and he explained that this was because of the implications of the 1986 Financial Services Act.

Indeed, anyone seeking advice on pensions or any other investment will find that almost every procedure that the adviser takes will be controlled by the financial services legislation. So, in order to understand what is happening, we need to look at the legal framework under which advisers operate.

1986 Financial Services Act

Until this Act came into force, anyone could set up as a pension adviser, without being subject to any formal system of control or monitoring. This *laissez-faire* approach to providing investment advice came to an end in 1988 with the implementation of the 1986 Financial Services Act, which has resulted in a comprehensive framework of supervision and monitoring of advisers.

Volumes have been written on the Financial Services Act and its accompanying regulations, and on its implications for investors and advisers. Here, briefly, are some of the main features of that Act as applied to pensions.

The Financial Services Act laid down that no person or firm could deal in, manage or advise on investments unless they were authorised to do so. The Act went on to define what constituted investments, and here there can be some confusion because certain pension arrangements are investments as defined by the Act, while other arrangements are not investments. There are a few exceptions, the main one being that journalists can write both generic and specific advice on general investment matters in their newspapers, journals and publications without being authorised, although they cannot otherwise give investment advice to the public.

Investments

All products and contracts marketed by life companies and unit trust groups are investments. This means that personal pensions, executive pensions, in-house AVCs managed by life companies, free-standing AVCs and annuities are all deemed investments.

If individuals have arranged their own Do-It-Yourself personal or executive pension arrangements, then the regulations of the Act allow anyone to manage their own investments; but if they are using their own investment manager, then he or she must be authorised.

The Regulations are unclear about someone managing the investments on behalf of a member of the family, such as a husband managing the investments on his wife's pension arrangement, or a son looking after his father's pension investments.

Non-Investments

- State pensions, both basic and SERPS.
- Occupational pension schemes.
- Deposit-based personal pensions and AVCs.

This division between investment and non-investment can lead to confusion over what advice can and cannot be given to individuals on their pension arrangements.

Authorisation

The procedures for authorisation to transact investment business are complex:

- Essentially, any person wishing to manage, deal in or advise on investments must be both competent and honest in his or her dealings with the public.
- The firm or partnership or trader transacting investment business must be of adequate capital resources and must maintain proper financial records.

These two very straightforward principles to protect the consumer have resulted in a veritable mass of rules and regulations, one outcome being that the individual buying an investment is virtually swamped with paper.

Polarisation

Investment advisers dealing in pooled investment products, such as life assurance and pension contracts and unit trusts, fall into two categories:

- company representatives
- independent financial advisers.

Company Representatives

These advisers/intermediaries represent just one life company and/or unit trust group and can only recommend the products of the company or group which they represent.

Company representatives can be either:

- Employees of the life company or unit trust group; these are known as direct salespeople.
- Separate firms, often trading under their own name, which have a sole agency agreement with one life company, which takes full responsibility for the investment activities of their agents. These representatives are referred to as tied agents.

The life company is responsible for:

- The training of its representatives.
- The financial health of its representatives in respect of its investment operations.
- Supervising the activities of its representatives to ensure that they comply with the requirements of the Financial Services Act and the myriad regulations.

Independent Financial Advisers

These advisers are usually referred to as IFAs. They have to be completely independent of any one life company and/or unit trust group, and deal with the whole market.

Accountants, actuaries and solicitors giving investment advice and transacting investment business must be independent.

IFAs are responsible for ensuring that their staff are fully trained and comply with the requirements of the Financial Services Act. They cannot receive help in the training from any life company unless it is connected with a specific product which the life company is promoting.

Advisers must either be company representatives or IFAs. A major firm such as a bank or building society can offer both services, but the independent financial adviser operation must have completely separate personnel from those employees who are company representatives.

The Financial Services Framework

The responsibility for the operation of the Financial Services Act rests with the Securities and Investments Board, known as SIB, which sets out overall policy and regulations for the financial services industry.

The main responsibility for running the various sectors within the financial services industry is delegated to three Self-Regulating Organisations (SROs) and to Recognised Professional Bodies (RPBs). These bodies are responsible for authorising firms, though firms can, if desired, obtain authorisation direct from SIB.

The involvement of pensions within the regulatory framework is widespread, as seen from the SIB diagram:

- Life companies and their representatives and Independent Financial Advisers are regulated by the Personal Investment Authority (PIA).
- Investment managers are regulated by the Investment Managers Regulatory Organisation (IMRO).
- The major banks and certain building societies have chosen to be regulated by SIB.
- The various professions – accountants, actuaries and solicitors – are regulated by their professional bodies. Many insurance brokers have their investment services operations regulated by the Insurance Brokers Regulatory Council.

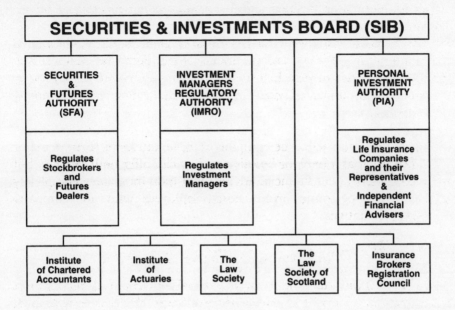

Advisers

Below is a list of the various advisers Charlie can consult and a brief description of the services they offer.

Accountants and Solicitors

They can give investment advice in-house to clients, providing there are partners with the necessary investment expertise. In all cases they must be independent advisers and must be remunerated by fees paid by the client.

The major firms will have separate investment departments or even subsidiary companies staffed by a variety of investment experts. Medium- and smaller-sized firms will have specific partners authorised to give investment advice.

Many smaller firms do not have the expertise to give in-house investment advice. They are not allowed to be company representatives, but can introduce clients to IFAs.

Banks and Building Societies

The major clearing banks and many major building societies have their own in-house life companies (referred to as bancassurance). As such, the bank or building society branch managers and their staff are representatives of the in-house life company and can only recommend its products to clients and customers. Most other building societies are representatives of a major life company and the staff at the societies' branches can only advise on and recommend the products of that life company.

Each of the banks and building societies also has an independent financial advice service which operates completely separately from the in-house or tied life company. The customer has to arrange through the branch to see a representative of the independent service, with such a meeting taking place at the branch or, if required, at the customer's home.

Registered Insurance Brokers

Most insurance brokers provide both general insurance and life assurance services to clients. In some firms, the life assurance operation is a stand-alone business, while in other broking firms the general insurance operations dominate the business and the life assurance is a back-up to the general insurance business.

In order to obtain registration, brokers must have passed the relevant insurance examinations.

Company Representatives

The life company is responsible for training and supervising the representative, as described earlier. However, the firm could well be trading under its own name, and therefore not easily distinguished from an independent adviser.

Independent Financial Advisers

Again this source of advice has been described earlier.

DEALING WITH THE PUBLIC

Charlie's accountant decided that he and his firm did not have the expertise to give investment advice, and so were not authorised; however, he could introduce clients requiring investment advice to an independent financial adviser. Charlie's accountant suggested that independent advice would be helpful in arranging Charlie's pension.

Charlie's brother-in-law from chapter five, Archie Foresite, has been arranging his pension contracts over many years with a long-established traditional life company, and has been completely satisfied with the service and the investment performance. He recommended the company and its representatives to Charlie.

Should Charlie follow the recommendations of his accountant or of his brother-in-law, and choose either an IFA or a company representative?

Company representatives can only recommend the most suitable contract(s) from the range of products marketed by the company they represent, and are not expected to refer to the products of any other life company.

IFAs are expected not only to recommend the most suitable products for their clients, but to select those products from the life companies that offer the best and the most competitive terms and/or prospects for those products.

For example, a client is seeking life cover to supplement the pension contract. If he or she is dealing with a company representative, then that representative can only recommend the protection products offered by that company. In many companies, particularly the unit-linked companies, the protection contracts available are not really suitable for supplementing pension contracts. Since an IFA deals with the whole market, he or she is meant to recommend the most suitable pension contract, which in this case would be a term assurance contract, and select a life company that has competitive rates, underwriting requirements that are not too stringent, and a record of a good, efficient service.

In theory, this should mean that an IFA can offer a better service than a company representative, simply because he or she covers the whole market. In practice this rarely happens.

This is because the life assurance market is so large, with over 150 life companies offering a myriad products. The IFA cannot know the whole market without a research department to help.

The IFA is responsible for his own training and has to find out for himself when an awkward technical point arises. In contrast, a company representative can provide a top-class service to his client without access to the whole market providing:

- He is carefully selected and well trained by the life company.

- The life company he represents has a complete range of competitive products.
- The activities of the representative are closely supervised by the company in his selling methods and in the recommendations made to clients.
- There is in-depth technical back-up to the representative.

The representatives of most life companies should meet these requirements, and have expert technical backing from the company that they represent.

Unfortunately, however, there are some life companies where the activities of their representatives still leave a lot to be desired, despite the efforts of the supervisory authorities to improve the situation.

In practice an IFA does not invariably provide a better service than a company representative. As in most situations, it depends on the character and quality of the individual.

Principles of Advice

The two basic principles in giving advice, laid down in the financial services regulations, should ensure that the client gets a good deal. These are:

KNOW YOUR CUSTOMER

The adviser must obtain all relevant information about his client – the client's requirements, financial situation and circumstances, and the future plans and prospects – before giving any advice or making any recommendations.

BEST ADVICE

The client's interests are paramount at all times. The adviser must recommend the contracts that best meet the client's needs and requirements within the client's financial circumstances. 'Best advice' imposes on advisers the duty to recommend non-investment products, such as bank or building society deposits, if this is in the best interests of the customer.

Charlie Seeks Advice

Charlie decides to take the advice of his brother-in-law, and contacts the representative of the life company to arrange a meeting, setting in motion a complex chain of events.

FIRST MEETING

Charlie has met the representative, Leslie Wisebuy, before and he is therefore somewhat surprised that, after the exchange of pleasantries, Leslie formally introduces himself to Charlie, states that he is a representative of the life company, which he names, and presents Charlie with a sheet to read.

Leslie is not being rude or delaying getting on with the meeting. The financial services regulations require all advisers, whether company representatives or IFAs, to clearly identify at all times which category they belong to. It must be shown on all notepaper, visiting cards, and be clearly identified in offices and branches. Company representatives must also clearly identify the life company of which they are a representative. Many IFAs have a distinctive logo displayed on their notepaper and in their offices. And at the very start of the first interview, the adviser must identify himself and his category.

Once Leslie has done this, he is then required to present Charlie with his official Terms of Business, which Charlie should read before continuing with the meeting. Company representatives and IFAs have slightly different terms of business and the format of the guide is laid down by the regulatory authorities.

The Terms of Business letter not only reaffirms Leslie's status as adviser and the company he represents, but contains useful information to help Charlie in dealing with advisers.

Leslie takes down the relevant details relating to Charlie's earnings, his tax position, other income and outgoings. Much of the information is personal, but without it, Leslie, or any other adviser, cannot make recommendations that will best meet Charlie's needs. A good adviser will not only ask what the client wants – often the client is not sure himself what he wants – but will endeavour to ensure that the needs of the client and his family are taken into account. For example, Charlie may only talk about setting up a pension, but Leslie will ask Charlie to consider also taking out life cover to protect his family should he die early.

THE EQUITABLE LIFE ASSURANCE SOCIETY

Terms of Business

1. REGULATOR'S STATEMENT

    Those who advise on life assurance, pensions or unit trust products are

    EITHER   representatives of one company

    OR   independent advisers.

    Your adviser represents the Equitable group and acts on its behalf. Your adviser can only give you advice on the life assurance, pensions, and unit trust products of the Equitable group. Because your adviser is not independent he or she cannot advise you on the purchase of products of this type available from providers other than the Equitable group.

2. The Equitable group is regulated by the Personal Investment Authority (PIA).

3. The Equitable group is bound by PIA's rules.

4. The product range of the Equitable group includes life assurance, pensions and unit trust products.

5. (a) You have a right to inspect copies of contract notes, vouchers and entries in our books or computerised records relating to your transactions.

    (b) We keep records of our business transactions for at least six years.

6. If you should have any complaint about the advice you receive or a product which you have bought please write to the Customer Liaison Manager at the following address: Walton Street, Aylesbury, Bucks. HP21 7QW. Telephone: Aylesbury (01296) 393100.

7. The Equitable group takes responsibility for any advice given to you by one of its authorised company representatives.

Charlie should check that the details taken down by Leslie are correct. If Leslie makes some tentative proposals, they should be put down in writing with approximate costings.

Above all, Charlie must be clear in his own mind as to why he is being recommended certain products, and understand what those products are and how they function.

Clients should be wary if the adviser tries to finalise the arrangements at the first meeting, or recommends a different set of arrangements to what the individual had in mind without setting out good and sound reasons for doing so. Above all, one must not be afraid to ask questions and must not be put off by evasive answers.

Finally, if the adviser recommends that any existing contracts held by the individual with other life companies should be terminated, then the individual must obtain a concise reason as to why this should be done, since termination of a contract usually means a financial loss, compared with keeping it in force.

THE REPORT

Over the following few days after the meeting, Leslie completes his report and recommendations, which he sends to Charlie. This report should contain a review of Charlie's current financial position, his existing pension arrangements, if any, and Leslie's recommendations for Charlie's future pension and life assurance arrangements. It should also contain the life company brochures for the various contracts referred to in the report.

Charlie should read this report, and:

- Check the facts in the report.
- Check that Leslie has summarised correctly Charlie's requirements as ascertained and agreed at the meeting.
- Study the recommendation and make sure not only that it will meet his requirements, but that he will feel easy with the arrangements. If he has any doubts, then he should contact Leslie and resolve them. Charlie could check the financial information on his earnings and tax with his accountant.

SECOND MEETING

Charlie arranges a second meeting with Leslie to go over the report, to clarify the final details and agree a final pension arrangement.

Charlie will then complete the proposal forms and arrange payment. If Leslie fills out the proposal forms, then Charlie should check the answers before signing.

Since Charlie requires substantial life cover, he will have to undergo a medical examination. However, this will not delay arranging the pension contracts. Indeed, some companies will accept clients at normal rates for an initial period and adjust the rates later, if necessary, when the contract is underwritten.

If Charlie, or anyone else making their pension arrangements, writes any cheques, then the cheques should be made out to the life company, not the adviser.

COOLING-OFF

Leslie files the documents with his life company. Within a day or so, Charlie will receive by post a bulky envelope from the life company.

The life company is obliged, under the financial services regulations, to send direct to Charlie full details of the contracts he is investing in, including, for pension contracts, details of the transfer values of the contracts over the first five years.

Above all, Charlie will receive from the life company a 'cooling-off notice'. Charlie, and any other investor, has the legal right to change his mind over the contracts taken out and get his money returned. This right is exercised by completing the cooling-off notice within days of receipt and returning it to the life company.

This cooling-off period provides investors with the opportunity to make absolutely certain in their own minds that they wish to proceed with the arrangements. This would be the case if the adviser had pressurised them into investment contracts that the individual did not really want or need.

DOCUMENTS

Charlie is satisfied with the arrangements so he does not exercise his right to change his mind. In due course, he will receive the policy documents from the life company.

Meanwhile, the life company arranges for Charlie to have a medical examination for the life cover and subsequent underwriting. In due course, it will tell Charlie its decision as to whether or not it will accept him at normal rates. If Charlie proceeds, then cooling-off procedures apply, after which he will receive the policy documents.

PERIODIC REVIEW

Charlie, and anyone in a similar position, must be prepared to review their arrangements, preferably once a year, and Leslie should automatically contact Charlie about the review. If Leslie subsequently gets promotion and/or moves to another area, then he should let Charlie know and provide details of the representative taking his place.

Susan Briteyes

In chapter six, Susan Briteyes decided not to join her company pension scheme but to make her own arrangements through personal pensions. She consulted an independent financial adviser on the recommendation of her father.

The consultation procedure followed a similar format to that for Charlie Easy-Going, but with a few differences:

- The IFA version of the Terms of Business presented at the outset of the first meeting was different in substance. Each IFA produces its own Terms of Business within PIA rules. The specimen is that from a leading firm of independent financial advisers.
- The IFA will not only be recommending contracts to Susan, but also the life companies to issue those contracts. So Susan should check from the IFA not only why those contracts are being recommended, but why the life companies have been chosen – in particular the investment performance and the financial strength.
- Above all, Susan must ensure that considerations of commission have not influenced the IFA in his recommendations. Susan will be informed how much cash the IFA will receive if she takes out a particular contract recommended by the IFA.
- The product particulars will disclose not only the life company's expense loadings on a contract, but also the IFA's commission.

This information on expenses and commission is provided after the arrangements have been completed. So if Susan is unhappy about these aspects or if she thinks the life company is charging too much,

Sedgwick Noble Lowndes

Sedgwick Financial Services Limited

Terms of business

Sedgwick Financial Services Limited is a member of the Sedgwick Noble Lowndes group of companies and a subsidiary of Sedgwick Group plc.

Sedgwick Financial Services Limited is regulated by the Personal Investment Authority (PIA) in the conduct of its investment business and is bound by the PIA's rules.

Regulator's statement

Those who advise on life assurance, pensions, or unit trust products are **EITHER** independent advisers **OR** representatives of one company.

Your adviser is independent and will act on your behalf in advising you on life assurance, pensions or unit trust products. Because your adviser is independent, he or she can advise you on the products of different companies.

The undermentioned are the terms on which Sedgwick Financial Services Limited (SFS) operates:

1) We offer independent financial advice but will not arrange or carry out on your behalf any business in which SFS has a material interest, without first disclosing that interest to you in writing.

2) Any instructions concerning investment advice should be explicit and given in writing, so as to avoid possible disputes. We will normally accept oral instructions provided they are subsequently confirmed in writing. However, we reserve the right to refuse instructions if they appear to be illegal or if giving effect to such instructions would appear not to be in your best interests. Any such refusal would be given in writing.

3) Authority for SFS to act on your behalf may be terminated without penalty at any time. Notice of this termination must be given in writing.

4) All documents of title will be registered in your name, unless you instruct us otherwise in writing. No document of title will be registered in the name of Sedgwick Financial Services Limited.

5) Documents of title may be sent direct to you by the insurance company or investment manager. However, any documents of title which come into our possession will be despatched as soon as practicable after we receive them and within the timescale set by our regulator. Where a number of documents relating to a series of transactions is involved, we may hold each document until the series is complete before despatching them. Pending despatch, documents will be held in safe custody on our premises.

6) You have the right to inspect copies of contract notes, vouchers and entries in our books or computerised records relating to your transactions. In addition, upon demand by you or your agent, and at your own expense, we will supply copies of entries in books and records relating to you. We undertake to keep records of our business transactions for a period of at least six years from the date of each transaction.

7) All money belonging to clients is held in a separate account. Client balances are segregated from our own funds. If we receive money from you for investment, we will hold it in our client account until we make payment on your behalf for the investments you have agreed to buy. If we receive money payable to you, we will forward it to the latest address we have for you by crossed cheque or, if you have given us details of your bank account and so request, to that account at your bank by telegraphic transfer.

8) The Financial Services (Clients' Money) Regulations 1991 set out a basis on which interest would be payable on money held on balances in client accounts. **However, as it is not our custom to hold client balances, we must inform you that interest will not be paid on client funds held for any reason.**

9) SFS may receive commission as a result of arranging investments or other products on your behalf and retains the right to share those commissions with professional intermediaries, at its discretion. For certain products, these commissions may be spread over a period of five years or more. However, in the event that you appoint a new adviser within five years of SFS arranging an investment or product on your behalf, any commission due to be paid during the balance of the five year period will continue to be payable to SFS, as part of its remuneration for the initial advice, and not to the new adviser.

(10) We will provide you with details of the amount of any commission payable to us on a life policy or pension contract and you will also receive this information from the provider (life office or investment manager). In respect of any other investments or products that we arrange for you, if we receive any commission you will be advised of the amount or commission rate. If we receive commission or any other form of benefit from the issuer of a security or from another intermediary, we will inform you but not tell you the amount unless you ask us to do so. At any time, you can request details of the amounts of commission paid to us on any investment made on your behalf.

(11) As an alternative to receiving commissions, we may charge you a fee for providing investment advice. Where we propose to charge a fee, we will agree with you the charging basis and confirm this in writing before we carry out any chargeable work.

(12) Unless otherwise agreed with you, when we have arranged any investments for which you have given instructions, we will not give you any further advice unless you request it. However, we will be pleased to advise you at any time you ask us to do so.

(13) SFS maintains a professional indemnity insurance policy for the protection of its clients in the event of negligence by any employee.

(14) If you make an investment which is matched by an asset in a different currency, or if an investment is denominated in a currency other than sterling, you are warned that a movement of exchange rates may have either an unfavourable or a favourable effect on the gain or loss otherwise experienced on the investment.

(15) In the event that you have a complaint about SFS's conduct of your affairs, you are asked in the first instance to write to the Regional Director at the company's local office. Alternatively, you can write direct to the Compliance Officer at our head office – Sedgwick Financial Services Limited, PO Box 144, Wellesley Road, Croydon, CR9 3EB, telephone number 0181–686 2466.

If you make a valid claim against Sedgwick Financial Services Limited in respect of the investments we arrange for you and we are unable to meet your liabilities in full, you may be entitled to redress from the Investors Compensation Scheme.

(16) These terms take immediate effect unless separate written notice to the contrary is given to you.

Personal information

(17) Any information you provide will be used, in confidence, to advise you as agreed. It may be necessary for some information to be passed to product providers in the course of preparing or implementing our advice. Product providers may also supply information to SFS about existing investments, but only if those investments were arranged through SFS or if you have given permission.

(18) We will not sell your information to third parties, but, occasionally, may pass information to associated companies within the Sedgwick Group if it is believed that this may be of value to you. If you would prefer that your information is not used in this way please tick this box.

all she has to do is exercise the 'cooling-off' option and start again.

If Susan is satisfied with the arrangements recommended, she goes ahead. She will need to review the arrangements, but perhaps less frequently than once a year – say every three years until she is older, in her forties.

David Short-Sighted

In chapter seven, David wanted to set up an executive pension arrangement. This is an extremely complex set of arrangements and it will need specialist advice.

David's first task is to ensure that the adviser is competent to make these complex arrangements. As we saw in dealing with David's executive pension arrangements, the adviser must be able to offer pensioneer trustee services and have access to actuarial advice. David should check on the number of executive arrangements that the adviser already has on his books.

David's accountant recommended a firm of consulting actuaries specialising in Small Self-Administered Schemes and hybrid schemes, and David accepted his advice. It requires several meetings to finalise the arrangements. David's accountant should be present at the initial meetings and the subsequent meetings where the financial state of the company is involved, and the decisions taken.

David must expect the arrangements to take some time to set up and be approved. But, like the others, he must ensure that he fully understands what is being recommended and arranged.

How are Advisers Remunerated? – Commissions v. Fees

Advisers, whatever their category, are not part of the social services system. They have to be remunerated for the services provided and there is only one source of remuneration: their clients.

There are two basic methods of remunerating advisers:

- fees paid by the client
- commission paid by the life company or unit trust group.

Accountants, actuaries and solicitors are remunerated by fees, since this is required by their professional bodies. But the vast majority of advisers, whether independent or company representatives, are remunerated by commission, and only a few IFAs are remunerated by fees.

Clients should not fall into the trap of thinking that because they are not paying fees to the adviser, they are getting his advice and services free. When a life company or unit trust group pays an adviser or representative a commission for arranging a contract, the cost of that commission and any other remuneration received by the adviser, together with the company's other expenses, is recouped from the person who bought the contract in two ways:

- By increasing the premiums or reducing the benefits if it is a traditional with-profits contract, or by reducing the number of units allocated on unit-linked contracts.
- By a charge made regularly on the underlying investment funds.

In each case, the individual who bought the contract is paying the adviser or representative indirectly through the life company or unit trust group.

In this respect, the terms of business could be informative to individuals in at least indicating the real situation. Instead, as the copy of each guide shows, they simply state that the representative or the independent adviser is paid by the life company or unit trust group.

Fees

When the adviser is remunerated by fees from the client, that client is paying for the work done and the services provided by the adviser. The fees charged can be either on an hourly rate, the rate depending on the nature of the advice given, or as an overall charge, based on the nature of the advice and the type of contract arranged.

When a life or pension contract is arranged, the life company either reduces the premium or enhances the benefits or unit allocation to allow for the fact that commission is not being paid.

A very few life companies do not pay commission to third parties such as IFAs, so their premiums and benefits do not need adjustment.

The main advantages of remuneration by fees are:

- The adviser is not influenced in his recommendations by commission considerations. The advice given by the adviser can include non-life investment and savings products, such as deposits on which no commission is paid.
- Since payment is based on the work done and the services provided, the overall cost to the client can be cheaper than the costs of commission, or the benefits provided larger, particularly when large premiums or contributions are involved.
- The individual receives a higher return if he terminates the contract early.

The main disadvantages of a fee system are:

- The client usually cannot claim the cost of the fees against his tax liability.
- Both the adviser and the client are watching the clock and the fee bill rising. As such, there could be a tendency to rush the consultations, thereby not going fully into the details of the client's needs or giving inadequate explanations. Or the adviser over-emphasises the advice given, thereby dragging out the time and increasing the bill.
- The client pays the fees even if nothing is arranged or completed following the consultations.

Anyone consulting a fee-based adviser usually has the first consultation free, during which the adviser sets out his terms of remuneration and the services provided. Individuals must make full use of this consultation to ensure they fully understand services and costs.

Commission payments are usually made in two forms for regular premium contracts:

- An initial commission payment when the contract is set up. This payment can be spread over the first few years of the contract.
- A renewal commission paid in subsequent years.

Both commissions are based on a percentage of the premiums or contributions paid, with the initial commission being very much higher than the renewal commission, to reflect the high incidence of expenses in selling and setting up a contract. On single-premium contracts, the commission is a one-off payment expressed as a percentage of that premium.

For example, the typical commission payments which an IFA would receive on a personal pension contract for Charlie Easy-Going would be:

- Regular premium – initial commission of 32.5 per cent in each of the first two years and renewal commission of 2.5 per cent in the third to the tenth year inclusive, nil payments thereafter.
- Single premium – 5.2 per cent of the premium.

Since Charlie was paying a contribution of £16, 440, an IFA would have received £5,343 in commission in the first year if he arranged a regular contribution contract or £855 if it was a single-premium contract. The commission on the single-premium contract represents a fee bill for five hours' work at £170 an hour – about break-even.

The client dealing with an IFA will be told in the product particulars details of the commission payments expressed in percentage form. However, no information is given on the remuneration received by company representatives.

Advantages of commission payments include:

- In theory, the cost of commission is meant to be spread over all the premiums paid during the term of the contract, whereas fees have to be paid on completion of the business.
- If the individual decides not to proceed with the recommendations made by the adviser it will not cost him or her any money. One reason why advisers claim that commission rates are so high is that the business which is completed has to subsidise the cost of the business not completed.

- Time considerations have less of an impact in the consultations. In theory at least, the adviser can do a complete job without being concerned about the ultimate cost to his client.

The disadvantages include:

- The overall cost is high for the large-premium contracts.
- Since the life company needs to recoup its costs by the time the contract is terminated, the benefits paid on early termination are low, often zero, if termination occurs in the first year or two.
- The temptation is always present for the adviser to go for the higher commission, particularly to recommend payment through regular, rather than single, premiums.

So how does an individual decide, given the choice?

Charlie Easy-Going obtained his advice from a company representative, so there was no choice.

Susan Briteyes went to an IFA for her advice. But since the amount of contributions involved was comparatively small, then she would be as well off leaving the adviser to be remunerated by commission, and she could have had problems paying the fee bill.

David Short-Sighted should pay fees for his advice on executive pensions. The contributions involved were considerable and he would be far better off financially paying fees, even though the hourly charge would be high and it would require many hours' work to advise and complete all the arrangements. Since he used a consulting actuary, payment by fees was automatic.

Any controlling director using an IFA to set up his executive arrangement should ensure that he pays by fees. If his adviser does not mention fees, the executive should insist on payment by this means.

For anyone else it is a matter of personal choice and knowing the facts. The most important feature is that the advice received is the best available.

Complaints

This is the era of consumer protection and both the pensions and investments arenas have set up systems whereby consumers can make complaints, have them investigated and, if the complaint is upheld, then to give redress to the consumer.

Unfortunately, but perhaps not surprisingly, a variety of complaint systems have emerged. The system which handles a particular complaint depends on the cause and nature of that complaint.

Pensions Ombudsman

The office of Pensions Ombudsman was set up in April 1991 under the 1990 Social Security Act.

The name itself would convey the impression that all pension complaints would be handled by the Pensions Ombudsman. Indeed that was the original intention of the Department of Social Security, which sponsored the legislation. But it ran foul of the existing complaints systems, particularly those set up under the Financial Services Act, and backed by other Government departments.

As such, the remit of the Pensions Ombudsman is confined mainly to handling complaints relating to occupational pensions, and anyone with a complaint relating to occupational pensions should:

- Endeavour first to get it resolved by the trustees to the scheme.
- If this fails, write to the Occupational Pensions Advisory Service (OPAS). OPAS is an independent organisation with a network of expert advisers who give help and advice free to the public on all pension complaints and enquiries, including personal pensions but excluding State pension matters. OPAS will first try to resolve the problem. If it fails, then it will identify the appropriate complaints system and help the individual make his or her complaint. The vast majority of complaints can be resolved by OPAS without requiring the adjudication services of the ombudsman.
- If a decision is required on a complaint, and the complaint falls within the ombudsman's remit, then his decision is binding on both parties, subject to appeal.

OPAS can investigate personal pension complaints, but can then only pass them on to the relevant complaints system.

Personal Investment Authority Ombudsman

Under the Financial Services legislation, all complaints against a member of the Personal Investment Authority in relation to investment business are handled by the PIA Ombudsman, currently Stephen Edell. Since personal pensions are investment business under the Financial Services Act, then complaints against life companies and their representatives and against independent financial advisers marketing these pension products would be investigated by the PIA Ombudsman Bureau.

Complainants must first endeavour to get their complaint resolved by the life company or financial adviser before taking their complaint to the Bureau and the Ombudsman.

If the complaint cannot be resolved by negotiation or explanation, then the Ombudsman can adjudicate, his decision being binding on the member – the amount of award varying with the type of case involved. In most cases, the maximum award is £50,000, but in others it is £100,000. His decision, however, is not binding on the complainant, who still retains the ultimate right to take disputes to the courts.

It is a grey area as to who handles complaints regarding company pension schemes issued and managed by life companies – the Pensions Ombudsman or the PIA Ombudsman. This is an important consideration for executive and company schemes. The two Ombudsmen have agreed between themselves on their areas of responsibility.

Most people would still be confused as to which channel of complaint to use for their particular case. OPAS would certainly direct any complaints received to the appropriate body. Complainants who sent their complaint to the wrong body would be informed as to the appropriate body to deal with their complaint.

Sex Discrimination

Individuals whose complaint relates to sex discrimination, in that, had the individual been of the opposite sex, then he or she would have been more favourably treated, can take their complaint either to the pensions ombudsman or to the Equal Opportunities Commission, or even direct to an industrial tribunal.

The majority of sex discrimination cases relate to unequal benefits paid to men/women compared with women/men because of different pension ages in company pension schemes.

The famous European Court judgement in Barber v. Guardian Royal Exchange ruled in May 1990 that occupational pensions were deferred pay and therefore men and women must be treated equally under Article 119 of the Treaty of Rome.

The addresses of the various complaints systems are:

The Pensions Ombudsman
11 Belgrave Road
London SW1V 1RB
Telephone 0171–834 9144

Occupational Pensions Advisory Service
11 Belgrave Road
London SW1V 1RB
Telephone 0171–233 8080

The PIA Ombudsman Bureau
Third Floor
Centre Point
103 New Oxford Street
London WC1A 1QH
Telephone 0171–240 3838

Equal Opportunities Commission
Overseas House
Quay Street
Manchester M3 3HN
Telephone 0161–833 9244

12

EXPATRIATE PENSIONS

Many employees spend part of their time working overseas, either within the same organisation for which they worked in the UK or on contract for an overseas firm. The period during which they work outside the UK can have repercussions for their pension when they retire, but it can also provide them with opportunities to boost their retirement income.

The situation is complex for employees working abroad, and it is only possible to outline the various situations that can arise.

William Wanderlust is a colleague of Peter Hard-Worker at Forward Enterprises, who is shortly to be seconded to FE (Ruritania), the company's subsidiary handling operations in the European Community. Bill, who has not worked overseas before, is concerned about the effect on his ultimate pension, and whether he should do anything about it. He has no intention, at least at present, of remaining overseas after this secondment is finished.

UK State Pensions

Bill's first consideration is the position of the UK State pension and social security benefits. The general position is that when a UK employee goes to work in another country, he or she has to join the social security system of that country – paying contributions and qualifying for benefits. But if that employee remains on the UK payroll, then he usually remains in the UK social security system for at least a year, before coming out.

Despite all the media hype about harmonisation within the EC and a single European market, the time when the member countries will have integrated social security and occupational pensions systems is way into the next century. However, there is a multilateral agreement within the EC which says that service in one member country counts towards the minimum period of qualification in another member country.

Ruritania has a minimum qualification period for State pensions of ten years. Bill has been paying National Insurance contributions in the UK for more than ten years. So he becomes immediately eligible to build up benefits in the Ruritanian social security system.

As matters stand at present, when Bill retires, he will be eligible for a State pension from Ruritania for those years he worked in the country, to offset the reduction in UK benefits while he was working out of the country. The pension will be paid from Ruritania in Ruritanian currency.

Indeed, if an employee has spent his or her working life in several different countries, under the present arrangements he or she could end up in retirement receiving several pensions from each of those countries in the currency of those countries, with none of the pensions likely to be very large. As yet, there is no system of interchange in place between the various member countries so that the employee can receive his whole pension from the country where he resides in retirement.

If Bill had been working in a country outside the EC, then the situation would vary according to the country concerned. The UK has bilateral reciprocal agreements with some 30 countries, each agreement having different terms. But the general aim is for the UK employee to earn local social security benefits while working abroad.

The agreement between the UK and the United States is materially different from the general pattern and must be considered very carefully.

The situation had Bill been working in a country where there is no bilateral agreement could have resulted in him paying social security contributions without acquiring any benefits, and losing out on the UK benefits. This loss can be restored at least in part, because Bill could pay basic UK social security contributions while abroad, or on his return to the UK could pay in a lump sum National Insurance contributions for up to six previous years.

Information on the social security position for expatriates can be obtained from the Overseas Unit of the Department of Social Security in Newcastle-upon-Tyne, details obtainable from the local DSS office.

Occupational Pensions

Bill is a member of the UK company pension plan, FE Pensions. He is now concerned about continuing membership of this scheme and the effect that working abroad will have on the benefits at retirement.

Bill should consult the pensions department about the position; the department, in turn, will probably check with their consultants over the situation.

In general, the Inland Revenue tend to take a very relaxed attitude towards UK employees working abroad as regards membership of the UK pension scheme, particularly if the parent company is a UK multinational and the employee is being transferred to an overseas subsidiary.

There is no problem during the first three years while Bill is working in Ruritania. He can continue his membership of the scheme. However, the overseas company FE (Ruritania) is expected to pay the employer's contributions to the trustees of FE Pensions, and Bill should continue contributions to the scheme. But this can cause problems.

Bill will be paying local Ruritanian tax on his earnings, and Ruritania, like many overseas countries, does not allow tax relief on pension contributions. Indeed, some countries could even treat the employer's contribution as a benefit in kind and tax it.

So Bill should endeavour to arrange for his pension contributions to cease while he is abroad and, if necessary, have a corresponding reduction in his earnings.

If Bill is abroad for more than three years then, technically, the Inland Revenue would require FE Pensions to take him out of the plan. However, if Bill has written into his service agreement that, even while working for the overseas subsidiary, he is ultimately controlled by the parent company, then the Inland Revenue would most likely permit Bill to continue membership of FE Pensions. The rules of FE Pensions should specifically state the position of expatriate employees.

The situation is more complicated for an employee of a UK subsidiary of an overseas multinational who is being moved overseas to another company within the group. Everything hinges on the control, if any, of the UK subsidiary over the other company in the group.

For example, the UK subsidiary may control the operations of those subsidiaries in other EC countries, in which case the Inland Revenue would probably permit membership to continue for the employee.

But if the employee is not allowed to continue membership, then he will have to leave the scheme, receive a deferred pension and rejoin the scheme when he returns to the UK, possibly on preferential terms. In the meantime, he should consider the savings opportunities available while he is working overseas that are discussed in the next section.

The main point is that employees should check on their position *before* leaving the UK.

Contract Expatriates

Adam Billder is a construction engineer who has worked on a variety of jobs in the UK, without ever making any arrangements for his retirement. He is about to go to one of the Gulf States to work on a construction project.

The amount of his earnings, tax-free, has now given him the opportunity to save on a significant scale – an opportunity available to many employees working abroad – and this can be done on a tax-efficient basis. The publicity on expatriate savings has concentrated on those employees, like Adam, working in the Middle East or other countries for high salaries and paying little or no tax. But the opportunities are available to anyone working or living outside the UK.

The facility for Adam and other expatriates not resident in the UK is provided by investing in a savings contract managed in what is known as an 'offshore' investment centre – a country that provides specific tax privileges so that these funds pay little or no tax on the invested funds.

The most well known of the offshore investment centres are Jersey and Guernsey in the Channel Islands, the Isle of Man and Luxembourg.

Many of the financial companies operating in these centres and offering savings contracts include names familiar to Adam and other expatriates because they are subsidiaries of well known UK life companies and other UK finance houses.

The investment of the offshore funds of UK subsidiaries is handled in the UK, but the administration of the funds will be handled at the offshore location.

Types of Contracts and Range of Funds

Adam is interested now in starting to save for his retirement. Some offshore investment operations do offer a contract labelled a pension contract, but it is not as necessary for Adam to invest in a specific pension contract as it would be in the UK. Such contracts are aimed at employers making pension provision for employees working overseas.

The pension contracts described in this book for UK residents are specifically designed to be separate from other savings contracts, because they have tax privileges over the ordinary savings contracts.

But all offshore contracts invest in tax-free funds (though the equities often have tax withheld at source), and there is no need to identify the contributions for tax purposes, as with a UK pension contract, because the expatriate, like Adam, is either investing out of tax-free income anyway or cannot claim tax relief from the authorities in the country where he is working.

So an ordinary offshore savings contract will satisfy Adam's requirements to build up a fund from his savings which can be used, if desired, to buy a pension. Indeed, for Adam, the major difference between offshore savings contracts and UK pension plans is that he does not have to buy a pension from his savings if he does not want to. Indeed, even on the pension contracts, the individual does not have to use the accumulated value to buy a pension. He can take it in cash.

The offshore investment firms have developed some very sophisticated contracts investing in a very wide range of funds, including funds not widely available to UK investors. The most notable of these contracts developed is what is termed the 'umbrella' contract. Adam finds that an umbrella contract offers him a choice of bond (fixed-interest) funds, equity funds and currency (cash) funds within the umbrella. The funds are not confined to UK equities, bonds and sterling cash funds.

Adam can invest in:

- A variety of currencies – the most common currency funds being US dollars, Japanese yen, German deutschmarks and Swiss francs, as well as sterling.

- A variety of bond funds investing in US Treasury bonds, Japanese bonds and European bonds, as well as in UK gilt funds.
- The usual spread of UK and overseas equity funds.

Adam can spread his savings between funds and can switch between funds. All these funds operate on a unitised basis, with the expatriate buying and selling units in the selected funds.

However, it needs expert investment management to get the best out of such a variety of funds – expertise which Adam does not have himself. Timing is very important when investing in and out of currency funds. Fortunately, the funds within the umbrella include one or more managed funds where the investment house makes the investment decisions.

Other offshore investment operations offer contracts that are less sophisticated.

Adam is concerned about the security of his savings if he invests in an offshore contract. Some offshore centres leave a lot to be desired in their supervision of investment firms. However, the major centres in Luxembourg, the Channel Islands and the Isle of Man do take their supervisory role seriously. This is concentrated, however, on ensuring that the businesses are adequately financed and well run, rather than concentrating on the complete protection requirements of the Financial Services Act, as in the UK.

Adam should play safe and invest with the subsidiary of a major, well known life company or investment house, where the parent company itself is closely supervised.

Returning to the UK

Finally, Adam will want to know what happens when his contract ends and he returns to the UK. He has a choice of actions:

- either he cashes-in his savings, or
- he switches the accumulated funds into a UK-based fund managed by the parent company of the offshore investment company.

In either case, he will be subject to a tax liability on the money unless he switches before he returns to the UK – in the tax year before returning. So Adam needs to remember to take action early.

- Or he can cease paying into the plan, but leave the contract to continue to accumulate value on a tax-free basis. Then he can decide at a later date, such as at his retirement, what to do with the money. By this means, he shelters his tax liability until a later date when, possibly, he is in a lower tax bracket.

It means that Adam must think ahead about his future plans, something that he, or most others, rarely does.

Advice

Adam will need advice in setting up the investment, in constantly reviewing it and, above all, when cashing it in. There are a number of advisers offering their services to expatriates, even to the extent of holding seminars and individual briefing sessions in the countries where the expatriate works.

Some firms have the knowledge and expertise to give sound advice. Others do little more than arrange for the money to go into an offshore bond, and collect the commission.

Selecting the best adviser is important, because the provisions of the Financial Services Act do not apply to advice given outside the UK. It is preferable for the adviser to charge fees.

However, the major international accountancy firms and the multinational employee benefit firms have personal financial planning divisions offering their services to both UK residents and expatriates. Adam already uses the services of a major accountancy firm for his tax advice and returns. So he decides to make use of its services.

Retiring Abroad

Many people on reaching their retirement decide to live out the rest of their lives overseas, for a variety of reasons. This is a decision that should not be taken without careful thought, including enquiries about payment of their pension.

Brian Settle and his wife Joan are retiring overseas. Brian will be in receipt of a self-employed pension, while Joan will receive a company pension. They want to make arrangements to have both their State and their private pensions paid direct to them, rather than have them paid in the UK.

State Pensions and Social Security Benefits

There is usually no problem getting state pensions remitted overseas. Brian and Joan can either:

- have the pensions paid into their local bank, or
- have payments by cheque sent to them.

In both cases payments are made either four-weekly or 13 weeks in arrears in sterling, with no deduction of tax. Brian and Joan will have to account for the tax with the local tax authorities.

However, Brian and Joan will only receive the pension increases if the UK has a reciprocal agreement with the country to which they are retiring that specifies they will receive these increases. If there is no agreement with the country, or if the agreement does not cover these increases, then they will not receive them. Their State pension payments will be fixed at the level paid on their retirement. Canada is a country where the agreement does not cover increases, and expatriates who have retired to Canada still do not receive the increases in State pensions.

Brian and Joan should check the position with the Department of Social Security.

Self-employed Pensions

The life company from which Brian purchased the annuity will normally make the payments net of UK tax, and leave the individual to deal with any adjustments with his or her local tax inspector.

Brian needs to ensure that he is not left in the situation of paying full local taxes on a pension that has suffered UK tax. Ideally, Brian wants to receive his annuity payments gross from the UK and then pay the local taxes.

The alternative of Brian receiving income net from the UK and negotiating with the local tax inspector can be an administrative nightmare. However, the first option of receiving gross payments is only possible if the UK has a double tax agreement with the country to which Brian is retiring. The UK does have such agreements with most European countries, the US and certain Commonwealth countries.

Brian should check with the life company or his local tax office whether such an agreement exists and then ask the life company, on his behalf, to apply to the Inspector of Foreign Dividends at the Inland Revenue for authorisation to make gross payments of the annuity. The payments are made in sterling and Brian has to make his own arrangements with the bank for conversion into local currency.

If Brian is also using other resources to buy an annuity, such as with the tax-free cash sum, then he has the alternative of buying the annuity from an offshore life company which would automatically pay the annuity gross, possibly in a more convenient currency.

Company Pensions

The trustees of Joan's company scheme are responsible for paying her pension, and normally, as explained in chapter eight, these payments are made after deduction of tax on the PAYE system.

A similar situation arises with company pensions as described in self-employed pensions. The existence of a double tax agreement enables the trustees, on behalf of Joan, to seek authority to pay the pension gross.

Trustees may be able to make the pension payments on a gross basis without Inland Revenue approval if the individual has spent a considerable number of years outside the UK prior to retirement. This facility could be useful if the individual is retiring to a country without a double tax agreement with the UK, and the trustees of the UK scheme are making full tax deductions to the pension.

Joan should inform the pensions department of her intention to retire overseas well in advance of moving there, so that her position can be checked and all necessary arrangements made before she leaves the UK.

13

WHAT YOU SHOULD ALSO KNOW

Life and Sickness Cover

Individuals, in planning for their retirement, should not overlook the financial consequences if they should die or fall seriously ill or become involved in a serious accident before reaching retirement, particularly if they have a family and dependants.

The benefits provided by the State social security system are on a par with State pensions – being totally inadequate as well as incredibly complicated.

State Death Benefits

These are the same for both employees and the self-employed who die before State pension age, subject to a satisfactory contributions record:

- All widows receive a cash sum of £1,000 on the death of their husband.
- Women aged 55 and over at the time of death of their husband receive a widow's pension of £61.15 a week.
- Women with no eligible children, who are under 45 at the time of widowhood, receive no widow's pension. Women widowed between ages 45 and 55 have a widow's pension based on a sliding scale from 30 per cent to the full pension.
- Widows are also eligible for a SERPS pension based on their husband's record.
- Women with children in receipt of child benefit allowance are entitled to the widow's pension plus an allowance for their children of:

- £9.90 a week for the first child.
- £11.15 a week for each other child.

The widow's pension is adjusted when there are no longer any children eligible for benefit, the adjustment depending on the age of the widow when this occurs, based on the benefits as if she had just been widowed.

State Sickness Benefits

Employees

There are two categories of benefits paid under the social security system for employees who are unable to work through illness or injury, namely:

STATUTORY SICK PAY/INCAPACITY BENEFIT

These benefits are paid to people assessed as being incapable of working through illness or disability, referred to as being sick. They are classified as 'contributory benefits', that is the benefit is only available to people who have paid sufficient National Insurance contributions.

But, as is common with most social security benefits, the operation of these benefits is complex. Paradoxically, the system is easiest to explain by starting with Incapacity Benefit.

INCAPACITY BENEFIT

This benefit is payable to people who either are not eligible for Statutory Sick Pay, such as self-employed people, or to people still sick when the Statutory Sick Pay benefits cease. There are three stages in the benefit payment:

- Short Term Lower Rate – payable for the first 28 weeks that a person is sick and not capable of working. The current benefit in 1996/1997 is £46.15 a week for a single person plus £28.55 a week for a spouse who fulfils the entitlement conditions.
- Short Term Higher Rate – payable for the next 24 weeks of sickness, the current benefit for 1996/1997 being £54.55 a week for a single person and £28.55 a week for a spouse.

- Long Term Rate – payable after one year if the person is still unable to work, the current rate for 1996/1997 being £61.15 for a single person and £36.60 a week for a spouse.

Both the Short Term Higher Rate benefits and the Long Term Rate are taxable, but the Short Term Lower Rate payments are tax free.

STATUTORY SICK PAY

For the first 28 weeks off sick, people in employment would receive Statutory Sick Pay which is paid by their employer. The minimum statutory payment is currently £54.55 a week paid to the employee with no payment to the spouse. Employers can pay more to employees who are sick if they so wish.

Statutory Sick Pay merges into Incapacity Benefit payments. Thus if sickness continues for more than 28 weeks, then people would be eligible for Incapacity Benefit, starting at the Short Term Higher Rate. For persons not eligible for the full 28-week period of Statutory Sick Pay, they would, on the cessation of the Sick Pay payments, receive Short Term Lower Rate payments for the balance of the 28 weeks, and then continue with the remaining Incapacity Benefits.

Statutory Sick Pay payments are subject to tax, unlike Short Term Lower Rate payments, which are tax free.

Self-Employed

Self-Employed individuals who fall sick would be eligible straight-away for Incapacity Benefit, providing they have the necessary contribution record.

COMPANY PROVISION – LIFE COVER/SICKNESS

As we saw earlier, most occupational schemes provide substantial benefits to the dependants of members who die while still working, both a cash sum, free of inheritance tax, and pensions to spouses, children and other dependants.

Many employers continue to pay employees when they are off work through illness or accident for some considerable time – a year or two – at amounts well above the statutory minimum up to full pay. Some employers complement these payments with schemes that pay an income to employees who are off work for long periods through insurance known by the inappropriate name of Permanent Health Insurance (PHI). Some employers even provide this cover, at a full or a reduced rate, to those who are not members of the company pension scheme.

If the company scheme carries the risk itself then employees are covered automatically for the total death and sickness benefits, irrespective of the health of the employee.

If the employer insures the risk with a life company, then employees are covered for the cash sum death benefit up to around £250,000, and sickness for incomes as high as £50,000 a year, irrespective of the health of the employee.

As we shall see, anyone providing death and sickness cover for himself or herself will usually have to provide some medical evidence. And if their health is poor, then they may well have to pay higher premiums or be unable to obtain the cover from a life company.

Obviously the death and sickness benefit provided by company schemes is valuable to all employees, but even more so to those in poor health.

Employers who do not provide sickness cover often still look after their employees who are off sick for very long periods, through generous early retirement through ill-health.

Employees not covered by their employer, other than the statutory minimum sickness benefit, and the self-employed should consider making their own insurance arrangements for death and sickness.

Self-employed and Employees

If the self-employed and employees with personal pensions die before taking the benefits, their estate receives the accrued value of the contract, or the death benefit, according to the type of policy. The contract can be written in trust for a named beneficiary so that the value does not suffer inheritance tax.

This can be supplemented by a protection policy, known as term assurance, which pays out a cash sum if the individual dies within a specified period. Again if the policy is written under trust the payment will not suffer inheritance tax.

The cost of a fixed amount of cover increases with the age of the individual at the time he takes out the cover. So cover is cheap for the young person but gets progressively expensive for older persons.

Individuals can pay up to 5 per cent of their earnings into a term assurance contract and get full tax relief; but these payments are part of the overall contribution limits for personal pensions.

The question is how much additional cover and for how long a period?

When Charlie Easy-Going was planning his pension he took the advice of his adviser and arranged life cover. He is earning £100,000 a year at present. So he decided to take out cover for £200,000 for the next ten years.

This amount, together with the value of his personal pension, would provide his wife with a tax-free cash sum and the potential value of the cash sum paid would increase each year with the rise in the value of his personal pension contracts.

After ten years his children would have grown up, and he feels that the value of his personal pension contracts would by themselves provide a sufficient cash sum for his wife. But he will review the situation from time to time with his adviser.

Charlie will need to have a medical examination for this level of cover, and the premiums could be higher if the results of that examination and his medical history show that he is not what underwriters term a first-class life.

If Charlie wants sickness insurance then he has to take out a PHI contract.

Executives

Executive contracts are company pension schemes, so they can provide full life and sickness benefits. However, the risk will have to be insured with a life company.

Executives, such as David Short-Sighted, in setting up their executive pension arrangements, need to ensure that the adviser deals fully with death and sickness cover in the recommendations.

Loans and Mortgages

One major drawback about making pension arrangements is that the assets in the arrangement are effectively locked away. The individual sees the value of his pension arrangements increase steadily. But, unlike any other savings plans, the individual or his dependants cannot touch one penny of that value, whatever their needs, until the individual retires or dies before retirement.

This is of particular concern to businessmen like Charlie Easy-Going or David Short-Sighted, who like to know that capital is available for the business should the need arise.

We have seen how David can arrange loans from his executive pension for use in his business. Charlie would also like to have a loan facility for use in his business.

Peter Hard-Worker, being an employee, is not concerned with financing a business. But he is still worried that the contributions he is paying into the company pension might be needed for paying off the mortgage or meeting the bills for school fees.

Indeed, David and Charlie would also like a facility to take personal loans, as well as business loans.

All three know that when they retire or take the benefits, they will have a substantial tax-free cash sum available. They are all interested in whether they can make use of this cash in some way before retirement, such as borrowing against the security of the pension arrangement and repaying the loan from the cash sum when it becomes available.

The answer is *no*. The Inland Revenue is adamant that a pension arrangement cannot be assigned under any circumstances, so the pension cannot be used as collateral for a loan or a mortgage. But, indirectly, there are two ways of getting loans on pension contracts:

- The individual can borrow against the value of the policy, and the loan is then an asset of the pension arrangement. We have seen this feature with executive pension plans. It is available on unit-linked personal pensions, but not on some with-profits contracts. This facility is only useful once the contract has built up to a sizeable value, so a loan cannot be taken in the early years.
- Many lenders will make loans to individuals knowing that there will be a cash sum available in the future, from a pension arrangement, to repay. The borrower may have to put up some other assets as collateral, usually the borrower's house, but with repayment coming from the pension cash or from some other source.

However, the Inland Revenue is most insistent that pension arrangements, particularly personal pensions, are not marketed for the benefit of obtaining and repaying loans, especially mortgages.

Pension Mortgages

The most common form of loan is that used to buy a house, known as the pension mortgage. The name implies something special about this mortgage, but in reality it is a quite straightforward mortgage, very little different from any other mortgage.

Charlie would like to move house in the near future, and his wife is already looking out for her dream house in the area to which they wish to move. If and when they find it, then Charlie is interested in a pension mortgage and how it works.

The operation is straightforward in principle:

- Charlie borrows the money, putting up the house as collateral security for the mortgage.
- He pays the interest on the full mortgage right up to the time he pays off the mortgage – known as an interest-only mortgage.
- He pays his contributions into his personal pension plan.
- Charlie would have to take out separate life cover, if he has not already done so, and assign it to the lender. This ensures that the mortgage is repaid instantly should Charlie die before taking the benefits.
- When he comes to take the benefits on his personal pension plan, he repays the full amount borrowed from the cash sum available.

The amount of the mortgage which the lender will be prepared to advance to Charlie will, among other factors, depend on the cash sum available. This can only be estimated on certain assumptions, such as the amount of contributions, the investment return and the age at which Charlie takes the benefits.

Although Charlie has complete flexibility on when he takes the benefits, lenders advancing the mortgage like to be reasonably certain that there will be a sufficient cash sum available at any early age, say when Charlie reaches age 60.

Life companies are permitted to prepare a benefit illustration on an selected investment return, besides the official 6 per cent and 12 per cent, providing that rate is less than 12 per cent. So the lender, if desired, can take a conservative view of future investment returns to ensure that the cash should be available to pay off the mortgage at a relatively early age.

A pension mortgage is a tax-efficient method of paying off a mortgage in that the contributions paid by Charlie to the personal pension get tax relief at Charlie's top rate. Effectively Charlie will have paid off his mortgage out of gross income, whereas with other forms of repayment it comes out of net income.

Some loan schemes provide for interest to be rolled-up and added to the capital outstanding, instead of being paid when it is due. Such schemes need to be avoided if possible. The scheme only works if the value of the contract grows faster than the roll-up of the interest, and that roll-up accelerates ever faster with time, such is the effect of compound interest.

Divorce

Throughout this book we have considered the benefits provided by various pension arrangements as they relate to married couples or a single person. But what happens when a couple split up and are divorced? What benefits are persons entitled to from their ex-spouse's pension arrangement?

The general answer, as we shall see from the following case study, is very little.

Diane, aged 39, is divorcing her husband Richard Flighty. She has two children not yet in their teens and is concerned over her whole financial situation, including her pension entitlements both from the State and from her husband's company pension scheme, especially as she has not worked for several years and therefore has no pension arrangements of her own to which she can look forward.

State Pensions

The State pension system operates sympathetically towards divorced persons who have not been paying National Insurance contributions. Diane will be credited on her National Insurance record for the period while she was married to her husband and he was paying NI contributions up to the date of the divorce.

So, in an extreme case, a woman approaching 60 who has paid very few contributions, divorcing her husband after almost 40 years married, would qualify for a full single person's basic State pension at age 60 if her husband had paid contributions over those years.

But this is not the case with Diane. Once the divorce has gone through, she is on her own in continuing her contribution record.

She should register until the time when she can start work and pay NI contributions. She can obtain a leaflet from her local DSS office and she should inform them of her position.

But she gets no credit for any SERPS benefits, even if her husband was in the scheme.

If couples divorce after one or both partners have reached State pension age, the position is that if one partner has a reduced pension because of an inadequate contribution record and if the other partner has a higher pension, then that partner will acquire the other partner's better record and move to a higher pension.

For example, if the wife is receiving just the married person's pension of £36.60 a week, while her husband receives the full basic pension of £61.15 a week, then on divorce the ex-wife will receive the higher pension of £61.15 a week. However, the wife in this example would not acquire any SERPS pension on her husband's record.

It is worth noting that the Department of Social Security may well take legal action if it was discovered that a couple had divorced so that the wife could receive the higher pension, but the couple still cohabited.

Occupational Pensions

Diane and her husband live in England, and the following discussion of the benefits relates to the situation in England and Wales. The situation in Scotland is considered at the end of this section.

PENSION

Until recently, the situation was that when the divorce comes through, Diane will lose all accrued rights to any pension benefits in Richard's company pension scheme. This has two major detrimental effects on Diane's prospects for her income in her retirement:

- She has not built up any pension rights on her own account and, unlike the situation in the State scheme, she cannot take any credit for the contributions paid by her husband and/or his employer. She has to start afresh building up her own pension and, being almost 40, she only has 20 years to do so if she wishes to retire at 60 – not really long enough to acquire an adequate pension.

When her husband Richard retires, the only claim to any part of his pension will arise if there is still a court order for maintenance against Richard. And if she is receiving maintenance from his pension, these payments will cease on Richard's death. This leads on to the second detrimental effect:

- The Inland Revenue, in approving occupational pension schemes, will only allow a spouse's pension to be paid to the legal spouse at the time the individual dies. It will not allow any part of the spouse's pension to be paid to an ex-spouse.

If and when Richard dies, the spouse's pension will be paid totally to his then wife, if he is married at the time. Even if he has no wife at the time of his death, Diane cannot receive, as a right, any part of the spouse's pension. If Diane was still financially dependent on Richard at the time of his death, then the trustees usually have the discretion to make payments to her – it depends on the rules of the scheme. But nothing is guaranteed. Even if Richard wishes to make financial provision for Diane, he cannot do it out of the pension benefits because, as we saw earlier, these benefits cannot be assigned.

However, their two children will still be entitled to receive children's dependants' benefits from the company scheme if their father dies while they are still eligible to receive the benefits – usually while they are under 18 or in full-time higher education.

CASH SUM

If Richard dies before retirement, the scheme pays a cash sum as well as a spouse's pension. Payment of this cash sum is at the discretion of the trustees, who have to decide:

- Which person(s) should receive a payment from the cash sum.
- If there is more than one person, how the overall amount is to be divided.

In making their decision, the trustees should take all relevant factors into account, the major factor being the wishes of the employee himself.

If Richard indicates that he wishes Diane to receive a specified amount of the cash sum, then the trustees would take this into account in making their decision, and almost certainly Diane would receive a payment.

If Richard has not given any such indication to the trustees, then Diane can still claim a payment from the trustees. But she will probably have to apply herself, or her solicitor on her behalf, with reasons as to why she thinks she should receive a payment.

The problems for Diane are knowing whether Richard is still in the company scheme and, if he is, what his wishes were, and how to approach the trustees having never had any previous contact with them.

For her own sake, and the sake of the children, Diane must keep in touch with Richard.

However, two recent pieces of legislation have set in motion changes that could improve the situation for ex-spouses in respect of pension provision of the former partner.

The Family Law Act 1996 has laid down the principle of splitting of pension payments so that the ex-spouse would receive part of the benefits accrued while married to the former partner. But while this in an important principle, there is no indication at all as to how this principle would be put into practice and how it would be implemented. The practical benefits for ex-spouses would still appear to be a long way in the future. But it is an important step forward.

Of more immediate practical relevance is the relevant section in the 1995 Pensions Act, which introduces the limited provision of 'earmarking' spouses' pension.

Under these provisions the court may make an order requiring trustees to 'earmark' part of the pension to be paid to the ex-spouse when the member retires from an occupational pension scheme. It may also direct trustees to pay part of the cash sum death benefit to the ex-spouse should the member die while still working, though this would not override the trustees' discretion for tax purposes.

'Earmarking' goes some way towards giving ex-spouses rights to a former partner's pension, though by no means a complete provision. To date, no court has made any such award.

DIVORCE SETTLEMENT

So what action can Diane, or any other person going through divorce proceedings, take regarding the loss of pension rights?

The only positive action is to ensure that the matter is considered in the divorce settlement, including 'earmarking', as mentioned earlier. Many people and their solicitors completely overlook pension rights in drawing up the settlements.

There have been one or two publicised divorce cases where the judge has ordered the husband to buy a pension for his ex-wife from a life company as part of the settlement. But the husband has to have the cash resources to make such provision.

SCOTLAND

Scottish legislation brings in pension rights automatically in the divorce settlement on the 'clean-break' principle of ending the marriage and sharing the family assets.

The Family Law (Scotland) Act 1985 lays down that the values of the pension rights of each partner are to be included in the family assets, and those assets are shared equally. This includes all types of pension arrangement, except State pensions, both final salary and money purchase occupational schemes, and personal pensions, including Retirement Annuity Contracts.

The value of the pension rights in a personal pension or an occupational money purchase scheme is simply the transfer value quoted if the individual changed jobs or ceased contributions.

At first sight, it looks as if the problem of pension rights on divorce has been solved in Scotland. But there are two major flaws in this solution. This is shown up if we consider the situation of Diane and Richard had they lived in Scotland.

The value of Richard's pension rights has been calculated at, say, £70,000. The other main family asset is the house, also worth £70,000; the remaining assets total £30,000, including the car, the house contents and savings worth £10,000. This makes the total assets to be divided £170,000; Diane and Richard should each get £85,000.

Now we come to the first flaw, for where is the money to pay Diane coming from? The Family Law Act does not over-ride the taxation legislation that states that the benefits in a pension arrangement cannot be taken other than on retirement or previous death, and neither can the benefits be assigned. So Richard has to find Diane's share of the pension rights of £35,000 from other resources; the only other resource available is the house.

The assets are divided so that Diane gets the house, plus half the other assets and Richard keeps his pension rights. Readers can decide for themselves whether this is a satisfactory solution.

This is the final settlement agreed in many divorce cases – the wife gets her share of her husband's pension rights through getting the full ownership of the house. If the couple do not own their own house, and have few other assets, then it is difficult to see how the provisions of the Act can be implemented in any way.

The second flaw in the position in Scotland is that the Act does not impose any obligation on Diane to use her share of Richard's pension rights to invest in a pension for herself. If by chance she has secured her share of the value in cash she could do what she liked with the money. In all other transfers, money out of one pension arrangement has to be invested in another pension arrangement.

Women in such a position as Diane should endeavour to replace the lost pension rights with some form of savings.

Other Means of Saving for Retirement

While a pension arrangement remains the most common and tax-efficient form of saving for retirement, there are other savings vehicles available both for employers to arrange for their employees and for employees to do so themselves.

Such schemes invariably involve the individual accumulating a capital sum, which can always be converted into income at the required time. These schemes usually have partial tax relief, but not the complete range, as with pension arrangements.

Personal Equity Plans (PEPs)

These savings plans are available to everybody aged 18 and over, and have valuable tax concessions. They invest in (mainly UK) equities, either in individual shares or pooled funds – unit trusts and investment trusts. PEPs operate as follows:

- Each individual can invest up to £6,000 a year into a PEP. Up to £3,000 can be invested in unit trusts or investment trusts if desired, the remainder must be invested in shares. The investment comes out of net income.

- A further £3,000 a year can be invested in a single share PEP – a plan that holds shares in just one company.
- Every other aspect of a PEP is tax-free. The dividends are received gross and there is no capital gains tax when the plan is cashed-in.
- The individual can take the dividends as income or leave them in the plan to roll-up.
- The attraction of PEPs to many individuals is that they build up a cash sum which can be taken at any time of their choice, and the cash does not have to be used to buy an annuity, as with pensions. As such, PEPS are a viable alternative to AVCs.
- Husband and wife can each invest in their own PEP.

There are innumerable PEPs on the market, and most life companies, banks and stockbrokers offer PEPs. Individuals should look very carefully at the charges and the choice of shares offered.

Corporate Bond PEP

The range of investments for Personal Equity Plans was extended in 1995 to embrace Corporate Bonds – the Corporate Bond PEP. Corporate Bonds are debt securities issued by companies, both secured and unsecured, which pay a fixed amount of interest twice a year and repay the original capital at the end of the period of the debt.

The Corporate Bond PEP can invest in the bonds of UK companies, except banks and other credit institutions, that are quoted on a recognised stock exchange – including sterling Eurobonds. Bonds at the time of investment must have a minimum remaining term of five years. The main feature of a Corporate Bond PEP is that it provides a much higher immediate income (tax free) than that provided by an equity-based PEP, but the scope for increases in that income and in capital growth are more limited.

Tax-Exempt Special Savings Accounts (TESSAs)

These are special savings schemes introduced at the beginning of 1991 and marketed by banks and building societies, with the money invested in deposits over a five-year period where the interest is tax free.

Most investors with TESSAs have now completed the five-year period. At the end of the five-year period, investors have the option of reinvesting the accumulated value of the TESSA – up to a maximum of £9,000, the sum of the maximum possible contributions on the original TESSA – in a tax-free account, but no further contributions can be made. However, TESSAs are still available to individuals who have not yet invested in the scheme.

It should be emphasised that neither PEPs nor TESSAs are a substitute for the employee making proper pension provision. They are top-up savings plans.

Share Option Schemes

These are schemes offered mainly by public companies whose shares are quoted on the stock exchange, to enable employees to buy shares in the company on very advantageous terms and so accumulate capital in the form of those shares.

There are several variations on the theme, but the basic operation of a share option scheme is as follows:

- Employees are given the right to buy a fixed number of shares at a fixed price at any time during a fixed period, which is usually between three and ten years. But there is no obligation for the employees to take up this right.
- Having bought the shares, the employee can sell them or hold them for sale later.
- The offer can apply to all employees or just to certain categories, such as executives and senior management.
- Maximum investment £30,000.

Consider the XYZ company, which has given a share option to its employees. Its shares are currently quoted at £3 a share.

The option is open to executives to buy 10,000 shares at the current price of £3 a share at any time over the next ten years.

Since the price of XYZ shares can be expected to rise over the period, the executives will tend to wait until near or at the end of the ten-year period before exercising their option.

Suppose the share price at the end of ten years is £13 a share. An executive exercises his option and buys 10,000 shares at £3 a share, costing him £30,000. But his investment is worth £130,000 on paper.

If he sells the shares immediately he will be liable to capital gains tax at his top tax rate of 40 per cent on the profit of £100,000 less the annual exemption of £5,500, leaving him with a net profit of £62,200. However, if he sells a tranche of shares each year so that the capital profit equals the annual exemption, then he effectively has a tax-free income, while still leaving him with the balance of his capital.

Savings Schemes

Employees can fund the purchase of the shares through a Save-As-You-Earn scheme, putting aside money on a regular basis with a scheme managed by a bank, building society or the National Savings department.

Under the SAYE scheme, the employer decides whether the option period is three, five or seven years, and the price at which the shares are bought at the end of the chosen period. For this type of scheme the price can be fixed at a minimum price of a 20 per cent discount on the current share price. The employee decides on the monthly savings within limits.

Share Incentive Schemes

Under this type of scheme, the employer essentially gives his employees shares in the company as part of the employees' remuneration. It has to be given to all employees, though the employer can restrict it to employees with a minimum length of service of five years.

The number of shares given to employees can relate to profits or be fixed. The maximum value of the shares must not exceed 10 per cent of salary, subject to a floor of £3,000 and a ceiling of £8,000 in the maximum value. Thus an employee earning less than £30,000 may receive up to £3,000 worth of shares, while an employee earning more than £80,000 can only receive up to £8,000 worth of shares.

There is no income tax liability on these shares at the time they are given to the employee.

The shares are held in trust on behalf of the employee for three years, during which time the employee receives the dividends on these shares, on which he will pay tax.

- For the first two years, the employee is locked in and cannot sell the shares.
- The employee, if he wishes, can direct the trustees to sell the shares at the end of the third year. Otherwise the shares are transferred to the employee.

GLOSSARY

Accrual Rate

The amount by which pensions build up each year in an occupational pension scheme – usually a fraction of an employee's earnings for each year of membership of the scheme.

Accrued Benefits

The benefits which a member of a pension scheme has acquired to date by virtue of the period of membership of the scheme and the amount of earnings.

Actuary

A person who has acquired special skills in assessing risks, such as mortality and sickness, and the financial implications of such risks applied to commercial operations. Actuaries are responsible for monitoring the financial operations of life companies and pension schemes. The Government actuary, among other roles, is adviser on the State pension scheme. Actuaries in the United Kingdom are Fellows of either the Institute of Actuaries in London or the Faculty of Actuaries in Edinburgh.

Added Years

A means of providing extra pension benefits in an occupational pension scheme by crediting the member with additional years of service in ascertaining the overall pension benefits.

Additional Voluntary Contributions

Invariably referred to as AVCs, these are extra contributions paid by a member of an occupational pension scheme, in addition to any normal contributions which are paid to the main company scheme.

Annuity

A contract bought from a life company, which provides an income for life secured by a lump sum from private funds or from the proceeds of a pension fund.

Appropriate Personal Pension

A personal pension contract that has been approved by the authorities for contracting-out of the State Earnings-Related Pension Scheme (SERPS).

Authorisation

Given to firms and individuals by the financial services regulatory authorities to enable them to transact investment business under the Financial Services Act 1986.

Basic State Pension

A flat-rate pension from the State paid to every person with the required National Insurance contribution record. It forms the first tranche of pension in an individual's overall pension provision.

Benefit Limits

The limits imposed by the Inland Revenue on the maximum amounts of pension and other benefits provided by a pension scheme or other pension arrangement. The limits may be absolute in money terms, or as a proportion of an employee's earnings, or both.

Benefit Statement

A statement or estimate of the benefits payable to an employee in an occupational pension scheme, usually provided once a year.

Bonuses

The form in which policy holders of traditional with-profits contracts receive their share in the profits of a life company. There are two types of bonus – the annual reversionary bonus added to the benefits, and a terminal bonus added when the policy holder takes the benefits under the terms of the contract.

Commission

In this context, it is a series of payments received by an insurance intermediary from a life company or unit trust group as a result of selling or arranging a contract of that company. The commission payment is usually a percentage of the premiums or contributions paid on the contract.

Commutation

The exchange by an individual of part of his or her pension for a cash sum. For pension contracts, there are strict Inland Revenue limits on the rate of conversion and the amount of cash.

Company Representative

An insurance intermediary – individual, partnership or company – which represents a particular life company and can only market that company's products. The representative may be an employee of the company or simply operating under an agency agreement. The latter are known as tied agents.

Contracting-out
The facility to opt for a reduced pension from the State Earnings-Related Pensions Scheme (SERPS) and provide the pension benefits through an occupational pension scheme or an appropriate personal pension.

Contributions
Payments made by an individual and/or the employer into a pension arrangement.

Contribution Limits
The limits imposed by the Inland Revenue on the contributions that are paid into a pension scheme or arrangement.

Controlling Director
A director with a controlling interest in his company – usually one who holds at least 20 per cent of the share capital.

Cooling-off Period
The period immediately after the sale of a life assurance or pension contract or unit trust, during which time the individual can cancel the contract without financial penalty. Most contracts have a statutory cooling-off period of 14 days.

Deferred Benefits
The pension and other benefits due to a member of an occupational pension scheme when he or she ceases to be a member of that scheme before retirement.

Defined Benefit Scheme
A pension scheme where the pension and other benefits are specifically defined, usually in terms of a member's earnings and length of membership. The contributions are determined, usually by an actuary, to meet the cost of the benefits.

Defined Contribution Scheme
A pension scheme or contract where the contributions, which may or may not be specified, are paid and the accumulated fund at the time the benefits are taken is used to buy an annuity. This system is usually referred to as a money purchase arrangement.

Discretionary Pension Increases
Increases in pensions paid by an occupational pension scheme made at the discretion of the trustees and/or the employer and not guaranteed in the rules.

Early Retirement
This occurs when an employee leaves an occupational pension scheme before the normal pension age and takes an immediate pension benefit.

Earnings Ceiling

The limit placed by the Government on an individual's annual earnings (currently £82,200) on which contributions and/or benefits are based for tax approved pension schemes or contracts. It is often referred to as the 'Cap'.

Earnings Limits

The limits on an employee's earnings on which the benefits are calculated in the State Earnings-Related Pension Scheme. Only earnings between a lower (£61 a week) and an upper limit (£455 a week) are taken into account.

Fees

A system where the adviser is remunerated by fees paid by his client, in contrast to remuneration by commission. The fees are usually assessed on the time spent and the work done by the adviser.

Final Salary

A defined benefit pension arrangement where the pension is based on the member's earnings at or near retirement.

Financial Services Act 1986

The legislation which established the regulatory system for controlling the operations of all investment business.

Guaranteed Minimum Pension (GMP)

The amount by which the pension provided by the State Earnings-Related Pension Scheme is reduced for a member who is contracted-out. Occupational pension schemes contracted-out on a money purchase basis and appropriate personal pension schemes provide whatever benefit is secured by the rebate, which may be more or less than the GMP. Other contracted-out schemes must provide a pension at least as big as the GMP.

Illustration

A projection, prepared according to rules made under the financial service regulations, of the future benefits provided by a pension arrangement based on certain assumptions as to the investment return and expenses deducted. The figures are not guaranteed.

Income Withdrawal

The facility for individuals taking benefits from a personal pension contract to take income from the policy each year, leaving the balance of the fund invested, as an alternative to buying an annuity.

Independent Financial Adviser

An intermediary who is not tied to any particular life company, and advises on and deals with the whole range of products from all the companies on the market. These intermediaries, often referred to as

IFAs, include registered insurance brokers, accountants, actuaries and solicitors as well as financial advisers. All must have the appropriate authorisation.

Inheritance Tax

The tax payable on the assets left by an individual on his or her death. There are a number of exemptions, including transfers between husband and wife being exempt of the tax, and on gifts made more than seven years before the death of the donor.

Inland Revenue

The Inland Revenue has a variety of functions beyond its known roles of assessing and collecting taxes on individuals and companies. In the pensions field two of its main duties are the setting of rules and limits under which pension schemes operate, and the approval and monitoring of all pension arrangements for tax purposes to ensure that they comply with these rules.

Investment Manager

A person or firm which manages the assets of a pension scheme or arrangement. The manager may be an external manager – such services are provided by merchant banks, stockbrokers, finance houses and life companies – or an internal manager such as within life companies, unit trust groups or the major self-administered pension schemes. All investment managers must be authorised.

Investment Managers Regulatory Organisation

The regulatory body, known as IMRO, which authorises investment managers, unit trust groups and the larger firms of financial advisers.

Investment Risk

The term used to describe the variation or volatility in the value of an asset – particularly applied to equity prices and property values. The risk is that the asset has to be realised when the value is low.

Last Survivor Annuity

An annuity on two or more lives, usually husband and wife, where the payments are made until the last person in the group has died.

Late Retirement

The term applied where an employee continues working after the normal pension age in an occupational pension scheme or the State scheme and defers taking his or her pension until later.

Managed Fund

A unitised fund where the life company invests in the complete range of assets and manages the mix or blend of assets according to market conditions so as to obtain the correct balance between maximising the return and minimising the investment risk. They are sometimes referred to as mixed funds. The value of the units varies in line with market conditions.

Money Purchase

See Defined Contribution Scheme.

National Average Earnings

The official index measuring the level of earnings of employees in the United Kingdom. It is published by the Department of Employment.

National Insurance Contributions

The weekly contributions paid by all employees and their employers (except the very low paid) and the self-employed into the National Insurance Fund. For employees the contributions are based on their earnings while the self-employed pay a mixture of level contributions and contributions based on their profits. The name is now misleading, having little to do with normal insurance provisions; it is more of a social security tax.

Normal Pension Age

The age at which a member of a pension scheme, occupational or State, normally becomes entitled to receive his or her retirement benefits.

Occupational Pension Scheme

An arrangement organised by an employer, including the Government and other public sector employers, or a group of employers, to provide pensions and other benefits to some or all employees and their spouses and dependants on the retirement or death of the employee, or on that person leaving the service of the employer.

Pensionable Earnings

The earnings, within IR limits, of an employee on which benefits and contributions are based.

Pension Increases

The increases made to an individual's pension once it has become payable. Such increases may be guaranteed on a fixed annual increase, linked to an index such as the Retail Price Index, or made on a discretionary basis. There may be limits imposed by the Inland Revenue on the maximum amount of the increase in the pension.

Permanent Health Insurance

Insurance contracts which provide protection against loss of income through an individual being off work through prolonged sickness or disability.

Personal Investment Authority

The regulatory body, referred to as the PIA, which controls the marketing of life assurance and unit trust products and the activities of intermediaries, both company representatives and Independent Financial Advisers.

Personal Pensions

Contracts issued by a life company or other approved financial institution which allow an individual, whether employed or self-employed, to make his or her own pension provision. The current personal pension contracts were introduced in July 1988.

Protected Rights Personal Pension

A personal pension contract effected by an individual to receive a transfer of the value of his deferred benefits from a contracted-out occupational pension scheme.

Rate of Return

The growth in the value of an asset through dividend or interest payments and capital appreciation. The return can be negative if the value of the capital depreciates. It is usually calculated on an annual basis.

Real Rate of Return

The rate of return over a period, usually a year, less the rate of inflation, as measured by the Retail Price Index, over the same period. If the real rate is positive then the assets are appreciating in value relative to inflation, and vice versa if the rate is negative.

Rebate

The reduction in both employees' and employers' National Insurance contributions applicable to those employees who have contracted-out of the State Earnings-Related Pension Scheme.

Retail Price Index

Known as the RPI, the index is the official measure of the cost of living, compiled from the price movements of a range of goods and services. The change in the index is now the accepted measure of the rate of inflation. It is compiled by the Department of Employment.

Retirement Annuity Contract

The old-style personal pensions, which ceased to be available in July 1988 when the new-style personal pensions came into being. However, existing holders of these contracts can still keep them in force, paying contributions and taking benefits under the old rules. They can transfer into the new-style personal pensions at any chosen time.

Securities and Investments Board

This is the main regulatory body for the financial services industry, set up to implement the provisions of the Financial Services Act 1986. Its primary function is to set out the ground rules for regulating investment services, rather than to monitor the day-to-day operations of investment firms.

Small Self-Administered Scheme

An occupational pension scheme set up to provide pensions for controlling directors and executives on a self-administered basis. It has very few members, perhaps only the one director, as well as its own special rules laid down by the Inland Revenue.

Staggered Vesting

Staggered vesting or phased annuities – the name given to the process whereby an individual on retirement takes benefits year by year until age 75 instead of cashing in the contracts at the time of retirement.

State Earnings-Related Pension Scheme

The name, or its abbreviation SERPS, is widely used to describe the second tier, or additional component, of the State pension scheme. It provides pensions for employees based only on each person's average earnings, revalued to allow for the average growth in earnings between certain limits. Employees can opt for a reduced pension from the scheme and make their own pension provisions, subject to certain conditions. The official literature always refers to the scheme by its official name – the Additional Pension.

State Pension Age

The age at which individuals become eligible to receive retirement pensions from the State pension scheme – currently 65 for men and 60 for women, but being age 65 for both men and women from March 2020.

Tax-exempt Funds

Simply, funds not liable to pay tax, either on the dividends, interest payments or rents received, or on the gains made when an investment is sold. Approved pension arrangements hold their assets in tax-exempt funds.

Tax Relief

The relief given to individuals and companies on their pension contributions. The relief may be given direct, in that the contributions are paid net of tax, or deducted from an employee's earnings before the income tax liability is assessed. Alternatively, the individual or company may pay contributions gross and reclaim the tax relief from the Inland Revenue.

Terms of Business

The official form which must be given to individuals at the outset of any interview by a company representative or an Independent Financial Adviser. It informs the individual of the status of the intermediary or adviser and includes details of the information which should be provided and the method of renumeration.

Transfer Value

The cash equivalent of the deferred pension; an employee who is leaving or has left an occupational scheme can arrange for this cash to be transferred to another pension arrangement, either a different occupational scheme or a contract from a life company.

Trustee

A person or company appointed to carry out the purposes of the trust in accordance with the trust deed and rules, and the general principles of trust law. As such, the trustees are responsible for administering company pension schemes set up under trust.

Unit Linking

A system of investment under which the value of the assets held in the fund is divided up into units of equal worth, and allocated to individual investors in the fund according to the size of their investment. The value of the units depends on whether they are being bought (the offer price) or sold (the bid price) – the difference in the two prices representing the differences in cost of buying and selling assets and in running the fund.

With-profits

The traditional method of investment in life and pension contracts, marketed mainly by the longer-established life companies. The contributions are paid into an actively managed fund which invests in the whole range of available investments. The life company takes its expenses from the fund, and the investor receives his or her share of the profits from the fund in the form of bonus additions to the benefits. The fluctuations in returns and asset values generally associated with investment in such portfolios are smoothed out in determining profits. The bonus additions, once declared, are guaranteed.

L&L&L&L&L&L&L&L

INDEX